CHILDREN AND

To Annie
with love
and thanks
from
Penny
Sept '92

A CPAS Handbook

CHILDREN
AND
EVANGELISM

Penny Frank

Marshall Pickering
An Imprint of HarperCollins*Publishers*

Marshall Pickering is an Imprint of
HarperCollins*Religious*
Part of HarperCollins*Publishers*
77–85 Fulham Palace Road, London W6 8JB

First published in Great Britain
in 1992 by Marshall Pickering

1 3 5 7 9 10 8 6 4 2

A catalogue record for this book is
available from the British Library

ISBN 0 551 02630 8

Phototypeset by Intype, London
Printed and bound in Great Britain by
HarperCollinsManufacturing Glasgow

Contents

**To Dave Richards
who first gave me the courage
to call myself an evangelist**

Preface

I have written this book in the middle of the whole process of learning about evangelism, taking up every opportunity to be involved in it and reading what other people have written about it. I'm sure that one day someone will write that definitive book on children's evangelism which will say it all. At the moment, there are many of us still exploring what God is doing among children and how we can be involved in that. It is not surprising that many of us are putting pen to paper – these are exciting times.

In the Old Testament many people came to points in their lives where they wanted to put down a marker. The markers were usually heaps of stones to which they could come back at a later stage, as Jacob did in Genesis 28, and remember that God had met with them there. Sometimes God told them to build the marker and sometimes the action grew naturally out of their response to him. For me, this book is a memorial stone to mark at this point on the way that God has met with me about evangelism and children. It is not the end of the journey, far from it, but a recognizable point where I want to praise him for what I have learnt and for what he has done.

Most of the experience of this book I have gained in the secure context of my own family. Many times in evangelism events I have been in the privileged position to look across the hall and see my son Richard working as a clown, further round my son Jonathan playing saxophone in the band, and my husband Thomas stuck behind a video camera. Yet to thank my family would not be appropriate; we have learnt this book as a family. All we are doing now is standing together round a heap of stones and saying in the language of the Old Testament, "God has brought us this far in evangelism and we are going on with him."

Part One
UNDERSTANDING
EVANGELISM

1

Real Children

In the four years that have elapsed since I was a primary school teacher, I have faced the enormous struggle of remembering what children are really like. I have taken opportunities to go back into schools, to be with children I know as friends, and to be with children's groups in my church. I have frequently been made to realize how quickly the image of a real child is replaced in my mind by a similar, but inaccurate, look-alike.

The purpose of this chapter is to make sure that when we consider "Children and Evangelism" we remember we are talking about real children. If that is not true, whatever conclusions we come to will be invalid and then, however frequently we explain the Gospel, it will never reach its target. The under-tens I have in mind are attracted by people, colour and bustle; they have energy which gushes rather than flows; above all they show inexhaustible curiosity.

It is this curiosity which I want to explore by way of introduction. Every subject is important to the under-tens and there is a list of questions for every subject. Most of the questions which small children ask are not answered to their satisfaction. Many of the questions would need a chemistry or physics graduate to be answered properly. The world to a small, secure child is a place of continual and ever-widening challenge. The smallest and most insignificant activity, like de-icing the freezer or changing the oil in the car, opens up for them the most profound thoughts and questions. One of the difficulties we have is to make the most of these opportunities for learning when as parents and leaders we are busy with a hundred and one other things.

I remember once using a loofah which we had been given

for Christmas. As I sat in the bath watching the new loofah puff up in the water, I realized that I should have given it to the boys in *their* bath time earlier so that they could see this happening. Their questions would have been endless because they would have been fascinated. So why didn't I? Well, we had had a day out; I had forgotten to take our meal out of the freezer before we left in the morning; I was tired; they were crabby; it never entered my head. Most parents, exhausted by the general wear and tear of just sharing a home with these characters, will miss lots of opportunities to satisfy the quest for knowledge in their children.

1.1 Questions – the way children learn

The place of curiosity in the early learning process cannot have escaped the attention of any parent. Surviving the dawn of language skills in my own small children seemed to require a level of patience and general knowledge without which I had happily survived as a teacher. Conversation between parents and small children is so demanding because the focus of the questions is so unpredictable. At least in the classroom there is some indication of the subject in hand. In the home or at Granny's house, on the bus or in church, it can be about *anything*.

Daddy . . .
"**Why** does the water fall out of the tap in that shape?"
"**Why** does rain fall out of the clouds in bits?"
"**Why** doesn't it come in the same shape as the water from the tap?"
"**Why** does Daddy make that funny noise when he is asleep?"
"**Why** can't I breathe water?"
"**Where** does the dark go when you switch on the light?"
"**Why** can't we keep the dark there all the time?"
"**Why** does the plasticine go soft when you hold it in your hand?"

"**So why** does the pastry go hard when you put it in
the oven?"
"**What** do you call those things your ears hold up?"
(ear-rings)
"**If** you kiss my pillow will I feel it when you've gone
out?"

1.2 Why are children curious?

Children are born with questioning minds. I remember
waking up early on one summer holiday. The clock said 5am
– not my natural waking time. The reason for my abrupt
return to consciousness was soon explained as I listened to
the father in the neighbouring tent. He was happily oblivious
of any adult audience and his voice could be clearly heard
across our quiet camp site. "Where do the birdies fly?" he
asked in a voice full of forced glee. He fortunately provided
his own answer, "Up in the sky." There was a pause while
a baby could be heard chuckling happily at this cunning
revelation. "Where do the daisies grow? Down in the field."
The question/ answer/ chuckle pattern continued for some
time while we drifted irritably off to sleep comforted only by
the fact that our two teenagers were fast asleep in their tent
and definitely past needing such early morning entertain-
ment.

That father was responding instinctively to the curiosity in
his child. When we look at a first picture book we say, "I
wonder where the dog is," or we hold something in our
closed fist and say, "Guess what's in my hand?" We are
basing our conversation on the fact that the child is going to
be curious about the answer. Many early games and conversation patterns would fail if the natural response in a small
child was "I don't know and I don't care." In fact small
children find their curiosity reflected in the games and
rhymes we introduce and they learn not only the answers to
the set formula but also to put their curiosity into their own
questions.

1.3 How are questions the pre-requisite for learning?

All these questions, whatever they are about, are an important learning process. In school, when a child asks a question about something practical which is happening, the teacher is really encouraged. After all, that means the child wants to find out what the teacher wants to teach them – that has to be good news.

The human mind seems to work by asking itself a continual stream of questions. Sometimes it can provide itself with the answers it needs. Sometimes, in a new experience, it cannot provide these answers so the child asks the question out loud. To begin with, these questions are welcomed by the parent because they are evidence of the child's natural development. However, after a while the non-stop game of questions and answers begins to pall. The questions of a young child are very repetitious and those expressed later demand answers using knowledge and vocabulary not familiar to the child – nor sometimes to the adult.

We need to welcome questions as being the surest sign of life, health and growth in a child if we are going to learn to communicate with them. Their fascination with the world and with God will produce questions of all sorts. They will look with amazement at the wrinkles on their knees which stop their legs splitting when they sit down. They will look in consternation for their lap when they stand up. They will want to know what God has for breakfast and who washes up after him.

Children who are not asking questions are either ill, or bored, or they have learned from experience not to ask them. This is as relevant a fact in evangelism as in any other area of communication. If, as adults, we treat ordinary questions with anything less than a welcome, we will find ourselves one day wishing they *would* ask us how the Spirit of God can live in a human life. Then we will realize that they gave up asking questions long ago.

1.4 How does this process go on in a Christian home?

In a Christian home, the questions directly related to faith should slide into the conversation unannounced. To small children the faith of their family is all part of an altogether amazing world. They do not see the divides which unfortunately, as adults, we are aware of. Faith to them is life, just like ice-cream, a voice they know on the telephone or the time when their television programme is on. That's why parents who do not share the Christian faith are often genuinely worried when they overhear conversations between a child and a Christian parent which sound as though the child must have been brain-washed. They find it difficult to imagine that faith can be so freely examined within a home situation. But as we will see in the next chapter – that is precisely where faith *should* be examined.

A typical conversation between a parent and child might sound like this:

Parent: Do you think you could stop banging your feet on that box while I'm driving?

Child: Why does everyone in London paint their doors a different colour?

Parent: I suppose they all have a different favourite colour

Child: But who chooses the colour of the door – they all might like a different one.

Parent: I expect they decide who is best at choosing colours in the family.

Child: Like you chose blue for ours?

Parent: Yes, that's right.

Child: And Daddy said it was up to you 'cos he didn't think it needed painting anyway?

Parent: Are these stupid lights going to say red for . . .

Child: Mummy, is it like when you chose blue and Daddy said that it was . . .

Parent: That's right – like that.

Child: Does the Holy Spirit live right inside you, Mummy?

Parent: Yes, he does.

Child: Does he mind the new baby being there too?

Parent: No, the new baby was God's idea anyway.
Child: Is he comfortable inside you?
Parent: Who – the new baby or the Holy Spirit?
Child: The Holy Spirit.
Parent: Yes, except when I do things that are wrong –
    then he is uncomfortable and so am I.
Child: Like having biscuit crumbs in the car seat?
Parent: Yes, a bit like that.
Child: Like having wrinkles in the sheet?
Parent: Yes, a bit like that.
Child: Like having sand between your toes?
Parent: What *is* this bus doing? Perhaps – I don't really
    know.
Child: But why don't you know, Mummy?

                        . . . *and so on.*

Of course, the questions about faith are going to be as demanding to answer as the questions about electricity or gravity. In all these areas we are dealing with concepts which cannot be seen in themselves – but their effects are intensely interesting to a small child. When we deal with these questions we need to be honest, even if we are only able to give a partial answer – dishonesty in answers is one of the ways in which a child is taught not to ask questions.

One of our main problems is that the child's curiosity is not expressed at convenient times. A friend of mine sat in the Good Friday service this year with her small son. In a moment of quiet meditation the child asked in a piping three-year-old voice "Mummy, *who* did you say died?" My friend quietly told him in a hushed voice, trying not to disturb the rest of the congregation. "And *who* did you say killed him?" The child relentlessly pursued the answers he wanted. My friend was really sad that they had disturbed the meditation of the service but several people said afterwards how the amazed tone of voice from the little boy had really brought home to them the wonder of Good Friday.

Once the flow of questions is acknowledged as valuable,

the process of building them into any contact you have with children will occur naturally. Not that you will start cross-examining every child within reach. Quite the opposite – you will actually start to leave space for *them* to ask *you* the questions.

1.5 How does this process continue in the church?
As soon as you are aware of the way in which questions and comments can flow about any subject, then the natural thing to do in the church will be to leave space for that flow wherever possible. You will look for visual or aural stimuli to provoke and satisfy curiosity.

When going to their church group, children might be thinking:
What's that music for?
Why is there only half a poster on that wall?
Where is the other half of it?
Why is my group leader dressed like that?
Where are the answers to last week's quiz?
Which of mine are right?
Why is that one wrong?
Where is the chapter which gave the answers?
What's the theme this week?
What's on the video?
Is there time to see it all now?

This process of asking questions within the context of sharing faith is a biblical one. The system of teaching young people by using a catechism structured on questions and answers is not a new one. However, in the case of the Passover celebration, for example, which was initiated in Exodus 12.21–28, the whole idea was that the *children* would ask questions and would want to know what was going on. In answer to their natural questions the teaching which God wanted them to receive would be handed on. Nowadays in a Jewish home the questions and answers are a liturgy but they are still there – as are the questions and answers in baptism services today.

1.6 Why does open questioning stop as adult life begins?
Does this process stop because our minds stop working that way? This seems unlikely since even as adults we remember the information which satisfied our curiosity much more clearly than information which came unsolicited. When we hear something which is amazing we often say, "I've always wondered why . . ." Our questions do not stop, they just become silent and eventually we do not even notice them.

There seem to be five main reasons why we change our tactics as we leave our childhood behind:
1 Our questions are continually answered unsatisfactorily, or ignored.
2 Our questions are met with derision by the adult or our peer group.
3 Adults present a "know-it-all" attitude and therefore *not* asking questions becomes synonymous with being grown-up.

And two which operate in the church:
4 There is confusion between
   - "doubts", meaning "I *don't* want to know"
   - "questions", meaning "I *do* want to know".
(I am not suggesting that doubts *do* mean this but that that is the way they are perceived.)
5 Question and answer situations do not naturally exist in our service structure – our clergy do not expect questions from the floor, mid-sermon.

It seems that the habit of asking questions becomes subdued by lack of success and finally stops altogether. We take on the traditional adult role of having superior knowledge in everything. It is impossible in this role to ask questions – you are supposed to know the answers already.

1.7 What's the result when an adult lacks curiosity?

- If questions are always unsatisfactorily answered, the mind stops thinking of asking them as a way to get information. This will happen when there is a lack of one-to-one conversation opportunities because of the absence of an adult or because the available adult ignores the questions. It can also happen when the answers given do not ring true – the Father Christmas/ God wants us to be kind variety.
- When the asking of questions turns out to be a belittling experience, then the child might continue to ask questions only in order to annoy and belittle in return. For example if a child has found out that genuine questions are laughed off, or even laughed about and repeated between a group of adults, then the normal function of questions will be discarded. Instead, the child will ask questions which will in turn belittle the adult, like "Why are you wearing that silly shirt, Daddy?"

  Sometimes the questions which are asked by small children *are* funny. Apparently I asked my father when I was small why he didn't take any change out when he put money in the collection plate. The fact that I asked him right there at the time when we were in the middle of our silent, Brethren morning meeting added to the humour of it. We need to learn to handle this humour sensitively otherwise we will quench the flow of questions.
- When adults are never heard asking questions but only ever heard giving answers, the whole area of questions is labelled as childish. In today's western society the child is expected to grow from childhood with rapidity. The main aim of many children is to be treated as though they had already grown up. Children see adults as having "arrived". It is, of course, very affirming for an adult to be seen as the fount of all knowledge but it is important to realize that the child does not exist for this reason – to affirm the adult. The child needs to learn as early and as gently as possible that adults are still seeking for many answers to their own questions.

- The difference between questions and doubts in the Christian faith is an area about which many Christian adults show confusion. When I went off to train as a teacher in my late teens I was terrified in case my faith did not survive the experience. I had heard so many horror stories of people who had come out of higher education having lost the lively faith they started with. As a result, I missed out on many opportunities to discuss my faith and to listen to the different views which were expressed vehemently by those around me. I was so determined to survive that I closed my mind to any questions.

    What a stupid thing to do. At a time of life when the mind is buzzing with questions, how stupid to suddenly see them as a threat to my faith rather than the doorway to a deeper one. The main problem was that I had not learnt the difference between questions and doubts – and I *had* come across James 1:6–7 which says that the person who doubts should not think to receive anything from the Lord.

- The average church does not cater for the curious mind – either of the believer or the unbeliever. Some churches are encouraging questions from people outside the church by running groups especially for those with questions about Christianity. Some churches are encouraging church members to explore their faith by giving them the safety and licence for questions – for example in Home Groups. Children growing up in these churches are likely to grow up with a different attitude towards their own curiosity and a growing knowledge of the right way to satisfy it. However, the children in our more traditional churches are more likely to be found sitting still and listening like the adults do.

Questions are one of the main ways in which we find out what we want to know and therefore grow in our knowledge and understanding. The Bible calls that maturity. Because of this, we need to make sure that we grow up knowing how to ask questions and how to find the answers. If we offer inappropriate education on any subject, it will not answer the questions which are being asked. Instead, it will offer answers to other questions which have not yet been asked and the result is total frustration. As one little boy wrote in his book, which was kept for Library Book Reviews, "This book told me more about dinosaurs than I really wanted to know."

1.8 Recipe for curiosity in the Budding Children's Evangelist (the BCE)

If, for any of the reasons given in 1.6, we have learnt by adulthood that asking questions rarely pays, we shall not encourage curiosity in children. This will affect our relationship with children and will also undermine the efforts we make to teach them about faith. If we have had our natural curiosity demolished in this way, we need consciously to build it up again.

Health Warning: You will never be the same again – neither will your evangelism.

Step One: Start with an ordinary situation in which you might find yourself, like waiting for a bus or train, sitting in a carwash, going off to sleep at night. Ask yourself as many questions as you can about the situation you are in, regardless of whether you know the answers or not. Be really hard on yourself and don't settle for two or three questions – you would not have stopped at even ten questions when you were a small child. Get the maximum mileage out of the situation before you go on to another situation and repeat the exercise.

Step Two: Next, start to do this during a sermon – not out loud. Let the questions just flow through your mind. Take no notice of the guilt which will probably start to flow as well. You do not need to feel ashamed of curiosity – you were made with an inexhaustible supply so that there would be no end to the learning process in your life. You should not feel that you are wasting time either, even though the questions at this point are not being answered. I have already said that asking questions which do not receive an answer is a frustrating experience. However, to make yourself produce a deluge of questions seems to be one of the few ways to break through the time block and make yourself think like a curious child again.

The learning process goes on . . .
One of the facts we have to recognize before we can allow ourselves to ask questions is that none of us has "got God taped". So many people want to feel confident that they know all about God; that they can answer *any* questions and know *all* the answers and that God will not take them by surprise. That is never going to be true and we all need to accept that.

. . . and on . . .
We shall always be in a situation where we are learning about God, and his Word, and the way in which he works. As we look at passages from the Bible which we have studied, and discussed, and prayed over, we realize that we are still learning from them. That is even more true about all the passages we have never studied in any depth.

. . . and on . . .
We have learned about God from experience. We have experienced him in an odd assortment of situations. We have also learnt about God through other people and as we go on meeting Christians and sharing our faith together so we go on learning and maturing. We are always on a learning curve and questions are a natural part of that situation.

1.9 How can I encourage children to ask questions?

As we teach and live out what the Bible says, continually asking and finding answers to our own questions, so the children around us will realize that asking questions about faith is acceptable. The important factor with all Bible teaching is that it should both provoke questions and answer them. If all we had from the Bible was answers to our questions we would grow slowly in our faith. The Bible provokes the questions too. Study of it leaves us responding "I always wondered about that" and also "I never thought of that before". That is why the continual cycle of curiosity is necessary in all of us. In explaining the Bible to children we need to do so in such a way that their appetite for more is continually whetted. We need always to be aware as leaders that there is more for *us* to learn – then that attitude will be there in our teaching. The practical ideas given later will aim to help us do this.

When we come to look at evangelism, the process of learning through questions is crucial. We explain the Gospel in evangelism. If the way in which we explain it answers a person's questions, they can come to faith in Christ. They will understand the truth. If it doesn't answer their questions, they will ignore it. As we provoke the questions and then learn to answer them, our evangelism with children is likely to become more fruitful.

1.10 How can we be ready to answer their questions?

- *Read and study the Bible*. We need to be people who go on growing in the Christian life. We must make sure that we never think we have arrived and learnt it all. We must ask God continually for a real hunger for his Word and for understanding as we read it. That process of learning should never end through the whole of our earthly life. I have all sorts of questions to which I have never found the answers – presumably in heaven I will know the answers. We'll be returning to this key area later.
- *Receive training*. Once we have become reasonably efficient and confident in our role with children, it is easy to think we can then simply mark time. But we actually need to go on receiving training and growing as a leader. Many of the skills required for teaching, entertaining and caring for children will not be acquired unless we set aside time simply for that purpose. Unless we grow in that way we shall not be confident and encouraging when we sense one of those questions is about to be voiced. Instead we shall be defensive and unavailable. Again, we shall look at this in a later chapter.

- *Read books*. There is a steady flow of books for children. Books written for children are the most enjoyable way I know to be made to think as a child. Then there are books written for adults about children. Many of these are in more popular form for parents while the approach of others is more suitable for students. There are also books available specifically about children's questions, like "Will my rabbit go to heaven?" by Jeremie Hughes, published by Lion. All of these help us to continue to think and develop as leaders.

- *Watch television*. It is probably the major influence in any child's life. You may think there are exceptions to this statement – because some parents are very strict about viewing or maybe do not have a television. The influence on such a child by other children spreads the influence of the screen. Watch television on a Saturday morning and see for yourself.

1.11 What kinds of answers are given to questions?

Having prepared ourselves to answer questions, we need to be quite sure what issues we are prepared to be dogmatic about, and which ones we can only express an opinion about. Sometimes we sound dogmatic simply because we are not sure of the answers, like the preacher who had written in his sermon notes: "Shout loud, argument weak." We should not make all our answers equally authoritative. Unless we are clear about this in our own minds we shall never be clear about it to children.

Children need to know:
- When we are giving them an answer from the Bible.
- When we are giving them an answer which is just our opinion.
- When we are giving them any quick, thoughtless answer because we do not want to be bothered with any more worrying questions.

There are people who think that the answer to every question should be open-ended; that to be dogmatic about anything is impolite. This is very confusing for children and will eventually lead to questions drying up. They will feel by instinct that we are keeping information from them. We must make the difference clear between the sort of answers we can offer.

Bible answers
If the teaching of the Bible on a subject, like why Jesus died, is specific, as in 1 Peter 2:24, we should not give a flexible attitude about it. Rather, we need to make this biblical teaching very clear because we are *not* offered an alternative attitude by God.

Personal opinion
If, on the other hand, the Bible outlines principles on a subject, like spending money, which we know Christians need to think through to come to their individual conclusions, we must make that clear. As leaders, there is no reason why children have to agree with us. We can explain our point of view and our reasons for our conclusions but we are not supposed to manipulate others into sharing them. As parents, we can influence our children through our example. In this way they should be able to see the sense of what the Bible teaches and the principles it lays down, as they see God giving wisdom about the issue in family life.

Thoughtless reply
We have probably all experienced the horror of finding that something which was said in jest, or off the cuff, to a child has been taken as a seriously considered opinion. Sometimes we do not find out about this until later when the child has rectified the misunderstanding. Then it may well be recounted as a joke.

When I was small I was fascinated by the cricket commentary on the radio. Terms like Silly Mid-Off and Short Leg conjured up fascinating pictures. My guess is that at some stage I asked my dad about these at which point the game of cricket was explained in detail. The game, it seemed, was played on a domed field to allow for handicap. The people with one leg shorter than the other stood sideways with their shorter leg uphill from the other. The people who were very tall could still play because they dug a Gully for them. Mid-Off was a chap who had played for a long time and was a bit simple but when they publicly called him "Silly" he did not find it offensive. A Yorker was this chap from – yes, York. And so on.

My dad probably thought that I would not remember something which was so obviously a joke. I expect I caught him on a day when I had asked one question too many. He probably did not notice that I totally accepted this fascinating description. Even now, when listening to the cricket commentary on the radio I have to make a conscious effort to imagine the game how I now *know* it really is, rather than how it was in my imagination all those years.

We need to make sure that when children ask us questions about serious things – not cricket – we are giving them answers which are worth knowing. They will remember the answers. They will not then have to put on one side the information we have given to them thoughtlessly, in haste, or because the real answer was more than we could be bothered with.

1.12 Conclusion

However much we study, learn and train, however much we welcome questions about the Christian faith, there will be many times when we have to say, "Sorry, I don't know the answer." My biggest turning point as a teacher was the day when I realized that I had not lost the respect of my class by saying "I don't know". Certainly, as a parent, I feel that I have spent the last 21 years saying just that. In saying "I don't know" to children, we are teaching them a deep truth: we will never know everything and neither will they. God, and his world, are too wonderful for that.

◊ **Look back**
1 When was the last time you felt desperate for information?
2 Decide on one improvement to the way you read and study the Bible.
3 When did you last set aside time, money and energy to be trained to communicate with children?
4 When was the last time you read a book:
   • about the questions children ask?
   • which had been written for children?
   • which had been written for children's leaders about children?

◊ **Look forward**
In evangelism we are not only communicating with real children but about a real God. That is why in chapter 2 we look at the way our theology – the way in which we think about God – needs to be what the Bible teaches. Our theology not only provides us with answers to children's questions, but dictates why, and therefore how, we evangelize.

2

Real Evangelism

2.1 Children discovering God

When children respond to God, they usually describe this in very matter-of-fact terms. A ten-year-old returned from a Christian holiday this summer and was talking about it enthusiastically. What he was saying was showing his obvious enjoyment and satisfaction. He talked about the bedtime groups where they had talked and prayed together over the spiritual issues they had learnt about during the day. "One night when we had prayed together we just knew that God was there. Some of the group were laughing but some of us cried," he said. "We weren't unhappy though. We just knew that God was there."

Another child after a special event at his church said gleefully, "I asked God to forgive me because of Jesus – and the Holy Spirit has stepped inside me." The conversation came at the end of the event. I felt I wanted to go back to the beginning of the week and start again in order to have more children who were that sure and articulate. When children discover God for themselves, they may not use the words we would choose, or the right moment to tell us, but we will find that evangelism is addictive and we want to go on being involved in it.

2.2 So what is our starting point for evangelism?

Our starting point must be to know what the gospel is ourselves and to understand how the Bible encourages us to spread that Good News in evangelism.

Look at how the gospel is described in Romans 1:2–4:
"The gospel he promised beforehand through his prophets in the Holy Scriptures regarding his Son, who as to his human nature was a descendant of David, and who through the Spirit of holiness was declared with power to be the Son of God, by his resurrection from the dead: Jesus Christ our Lord.

Look at how evangelism is described in verses 5 and 6:
"Through him and for his name's sake, we received grace and apostleship to call people from among all the Gentiles to the obedience that comes from faith. And you also are among those who are called to belong to Jesus Christ."

In the recent launch into ten years of evangelistic effort, members of the church have started to call an assortment of activities "evangelistic". Although there is certainly hardly a limit as to what means can be used to spread the gospel, in evangelism we have to check that that is ultimately what we are spreading. If we are unsure about what the gospel or evangelism is, we are unlikely to be involved in either.

Look at the Good News:
• What is evangelism?
• What is the gospel?

• *Evangelism*
Evangelism is bringing people face to face with Jesus Christ because he died for them. It is showing people the way to God the Father, through the preaching about Jesus, by the power of the Holy Spirit.

It is confronting people with his name, his teaching, his promises, his life, his death, his resurrection and his kingdom.

It brings people into the fellowship of the church through a conscious decision on their part as they respond to what they have heard.

● *The gospel*
God became a human being in Jesus Christ.
Jesus died for our sins.
Jesus was raised from the dead by the power of God.

So, if it's so simple, what are the problems? Do you find that your mind fills with them when anyone asks you to consider being involved in any evangelism? Mine does. These problems are not dispelled when church leaders try to launch their congregations into evangelism on the grounds of duty and "oughtness", even though there are times when we are involved solely out of obedience to God. However, the sole result of this approach is to make the rest of us feel guilty – which just compounds the situation. The problems we all have with evangelism are real problems and they need to be thought about – not blundered through or ignored. The best way in which to be involved in evangelism is when we are motivated by an overflowing heart. This does not happen by the forceful arguments of a preacher but by the relationship we have with God.

To be ready for evangelism we need the answers to these questions:
● How do I explain my faith to another person who has no knowledge of the Bible?
● How do I know when it is the right time in a conversation to say something about my faith?
● What do I do if people don't understand the words I am using and stop listening to what I am saying?
● How much do I need to know and to understand before I start?

- What happens when I "blow it" and don't live up to what I have been saying?
- Suppose I can't answer all their questions?
- What will I do if they know their own religion better than I do?
- What will I do if they know the Bible better than I do?
- What will I do if they come to faith in Christ and then want to come to my boring, unhelpful church with me?

Evangelism for children must always be a long-term commitment otherwise we will find ourselves putting pressure on them for quick responses. Evangelism always is slow and steady work. Of course, there have been the great revivals but these have always been the exceptions rather than the rule. Jesus prepared people for the hardship of spreading the Word. He told his followers not to be surprised when they were imprisoned and punished for preaching the truth – that this should be regarded as normal. In our day, this negative attitude is more likely to be expressed as a silent resistance. Our neighbours and colleagues are more likely to respond with "I can't be bothered with religion" rather than reporting us to the secret police. The first disciples experienced both.

"When you go into a town and are not welcomed, go into its streets and say, Even the dust of your town that sticks to our feet we wipe off against you.

Yet be sure of this: The kingdom of God is near.

I tell you, it will be more bearable on that day for Sodom than for that town."

Luke 10:10–12

2.3 What is our starting point for evangelism with children?
The questions which daunt us about any kind of evangelism
will be the ones we find ourselves asking when reaching out
to children – and then some extra ones too. Anyone who
chooses evangelism with children rather than adults will find
that they have chosen the tougher option. The fact is that
many of the problems which may stop us reaching out in
evangelism to adults, also come into operation when we
approach children. It is important that we all face the fact
that evangelism will never be easy for the church. The situation with children is further complicated by other issues
which will be discussed throughout this book.

**We may find ourselves talking to children from a wide
variety of backgrounds:**
● children from an active Christian home
  – who have been baptized
● children from a nominal Christian home
  – who have been baptized
● children from an unbelieving home
  – who have been baptized
● children from an active Christian home
  – who have not been baptized
● children from a nominal Christian home
  – who have not been baptized
● children from a unbelieving home
  – who have not been baptized

Teaching such a variety of children may feel like a very
complicated situation. How can we make sure that what we
say is relevant so that they can clearly hear that the gospel
is for them? Does God love everyone in that list in the same
way or are some people more important than others? If everyone is the same then why did he choose some people to be
his "special people" and others who were not?
   Read through the book of Jonah for some answers. It only
takes five minutes to read. There we find God going to

extraordinary lengths to send the message of repentance and forgiveness to the city of Nineveh. This was a unbelieving city but it was still full of people God had created. God makes clear to poor Jonah his love for those people and his great desire for them to repent. When they repented, God forgave them. Jonah, the Israelite, did not understand why God did not bring down the threatened judgement on these pagan people – even though he had suspected what would happen.

God saw the people of Nineveh and Israel very differently but he loved them all because they were people of his creation. The message God sent to them through Jonah was the same. Jonah had to tell the people of Israel and Nineveh that God hates sin and that he would punish those who deliberately continued to disobey him. God may see the children of Christian parents and those of unbelieving parents very differently but he loves them all because they are the people of his creation. The message to them is the same. It is one of repentance and trust in him.

If up to now you have felt like leaving the whole area of Christianity and children to someone else, no one could blame you. Perhaps it has sounded complicated. But please don't give up. God asks us to tell the message he has given. We can obey by telling the message as carefully as possible – and leave the problems to him.

● *Children need to hear – because everyone does.*
Unless we start to think of children as part of a society which needs evangelizing *now* and stop thinking of them only as candidates for the future, we will be discriminating against children. Children need to hear the gospel because everyone needs to hear.

If we read Matthew 28:16–20 but then start to say children are the exception to that great commission, then why not find other exceptions, too? We will begin to say that people who have special needs because of a physical, emotional or mental disability must be excluded from evangelism. Then it will be those who can't understand (the uneducated), those who can't contribute (the poor), those who are different in background (different races), and those who are a different gender from the apostles.

● *Children need the opportunity to tell – because everyone does.*
Next, Christian children need our encouragement to tell the gospel to their peer group. Of course, they will learn from adult Christians that we are supposed to tell other people about Jesus. They will learn that they also are on the receiving end of the Great Commission. If, however, there is nothing happening at church to which they can invite their friends, then we are likely to succeed only in making them feel as guilty as we do about not speaking of our faith. Guilt is very debilitating. It never leads to creative action.

● *Children need to hear the whole truth and not a watered down pulped version – because everyone does.*
The third stage in our thinking will cause us to look at what we have taught these Christian children. Do we really expect them to explain and live out the Christian life for other children, when all we have told them is a few Bible stories? Have we honestly modelled the Christian life for them, and given them the chance to express doubts, difficulties and spiritual hunger?

Have we taught them what the Bible teaches about sin, forgiveness, punishment, the life, fruit and gifts of the Holy Spirit, the attack of God's enemy? Or have we merely presented them with a watered-down version of these things, promising ourselves to give them the full truth on their eighteenth birthday? If that is the case, we should be seriously worried when we send them out as young evangelists. They will not survive.

● *The church needs to exercise the skill of explaining the gospel to children.*
This brings us to the problem the rest of the church has in understanding the gospel. Many people who have difficulty in explaining their faith, go to help with the children because they think that will be easier. Many clergy encourage this attitude by saying, "Start with the children – you can't do

much harm there." They then back away from any difficulties
by saying they are there to help and not to teach. Helpers
are fine in that there is always the need for extra pairs of
hands but it evades the main issue – who *will* teach the
gospel to children?

Some people refuse to become involved in evangelism with
children because of the debate about the faith of a child
which has occupied the minds of some Christians over recent
years:

• do children belong in the Kingdom until they decide to
  leave?
• are all children outside the Kingdom until they decide to
  join?
• what difference does baptism make?
• what is being said by the different faith development
  theories?
• is there any way in which our theology and these theories
  can make sense?

To some extent these issues will always be open for debate.
The Bible does not give us one specific passage where
the answers are systematically given and the doctrine of
children in the kingdom of God expounded. Instead, as
with many other issues, the Bible teaches us about basic
attitudes.

2.4 What does the Bible teach about children and God?
The Bible does teach us about children, family and faith
issues. For example, we are able to see how the Old Testament rules for family life show some of the attitudes which
God was nurturing in his people. After all, we only actually
have one God who made one Covenant with his creation. If
we look at the way God operates in the Old Testament, we
shall have a very good idea of how he operates now because
God never changes. The Old Testament helps us to function
as parents and leaders of children now. The Old Covenant
was not superseded by the New but was fulfilled in it. In
this way, the church is included in the Covenant God made

with his people. When Jesus came he opened the way which until then had been open only to his chosen people.

God wanted the children of the adults he had rescued from Egypt to know what he had brought the people through:

"Remember today that your children were not the ones who saw and experienced the discipline of the Lord: his majesty, his mighty hand, his outstretched arm; the signs he performed and the things he did . . . It was not your children who saw the things he did for you in the desert . . . But it was your own eyes that saw all these great things the Lord has done . . . Teach them to your children, talking about them when you sit at home and when you walk along the road, when you lie down and when you get up."

(Deuteronomy 11: 2, 3, 5, 7, 19)

The making of the Covenant only made sense within the context of God's people. However, judging by their subsequent rebellion, there were some who were deeply aware of the presence of God and their desire to serve him. There were others who found God's pronouncements a real intrusion into their lives – they had only left Egypt because their family or friends had. This was presumably God's problem and not Moses'. The only way in which it became a problem for Moses was in the behaviour which this attitude produced. God, in taking the initiative, bore in mind the variety of attitudes which this motley group had towards him and he still made a Covenant *with all of them and all their children*. He also worked for change in them all – including Moses.

God's long-term promise to his people to love them and to be their God was in one sense unconditional. The only reason he gives for loving them in Deuteronomy 7.7–8 is that he loves them. That's the only reason God ever gives. But God made it clear to the people that if they wanted to prosper, their agreement to obey God had to be unconditional, too. This really sums up the Old Testament Covenant. The Covenant is the promise of grace on the part of the sovereign God whose word is never broken. God promises unconditionally to bless his people and expects them to obey him unconditionally.

Moses reminds the people as the Covenant is made:
"Carefully follow the terms of this covenant so that you may prosper in everything you do. All of you are standing today in the presence of the Lord your God – your leaders and chief men, your elders and officials, and all the other men of Israel, *together with your children* and your wives, and the aliens living in your camps who chop your wood and carry your water. You are standing here in order to enter into a covenant with the Lord your God, a covenant the Lord is making with you this day and sealing with an oath, to confirm you this day as his people, that he may be your God as he promised you and as he swore to you fathers, Abraham, Isaac and Jacob. I am making this covenant with its oath, *not only with you who are standing here with us today in the presence of the Lord our God but also with those who are not here today.*"

(Deuteronomy 29:9–15)

If you look at the words in italics in the Bible passage you will notice that the children were there at the time the Covenant was made. It was made clear that the Covenant was between God and them also. The future generations were recognized as being there too. The great-grandchildren of the children who were standing there (who were too young even to know that they might be parents one day) were included in that Covenant – and so am I, and so are my children. That is because the Covenant stands for all time and cannot be broken because God has made it and his word stands forever.

With Jesus, the way to God was open to anyone who accepted God's conditions; anyone who agreed to come by confession and forgiveness into the Covenant position.

Now because it was for everyone, it was called the New Covenant.

The Passover is replaced by Communion service, and in Mark 12:33, the Ten Commandments are summed up by Jesus as "Love God with all your heart, with all your understanding and with all your strength and love your neighbour as yourself".

Passages like these should help us a lot when we are trying to understand the position of children in the kingdom of God. Suppose, for example, we are looking at children of Christian parents who are being brought up in a Christian home. We realize from this passage that until the child reaches an age when individual response can be made, the child is contained within the faith and trust of the parents. There was in fact no flexibility for argument about the situation – the child was included within the faith of the family. They were there at the time when God said, "You are my people – worship me." God sees the children of his people as being within his covenant with his people. Those children need to come to recognize who they are and to live within the Covenant agreement which God has initiated.

The important principle which Jesus re-established was that God saw children as important in their own right too – not just as part of their family. When the children came to Jesus, the disciples tried to turn them away thinking that if their family was represented there that was all that mattered. But Jesus not only said that the children themselves should come but that the adults had missed the point; they had to come like children if they were to come at all. He says in Mark 10.14 that "The kingdom of Heaven belongs to these and to those like them". So Jesus reformed the position of children in society – they could come to God themselves and in coming they would set the vital pattern which others would need to follow.

2.5 Faith development theories

Faith development theories like those of Fowler, Westerhoff, Piaget and Menninger vary considerably not simply in the vocabulary and terms which describe the different stages of faith, but in their conclusions. Some of these conclusions were changed by the psychologists themselves later in their own professional lives. What seems to be clear is that people develop in faith in much the same way as they develop in any other area of their lives.

For example, John Westerhoff looks at what we call conversion as one point of a developing and gradual process which is likely to reach its peak in late teenage years. He would not therefore be involved in evangelism with children at all.

For Westerhoff, conversion is a point of change in a whole process of nurture and growth; a point at which the faith of childhood becomes "owned" by the young adult.

Our outreach to children in that case is seen as preparing the ground to help them develop through a period of searching for a later owned faith. He would also see us operating within the childhood characteristic of joining and belonging to a group. The child's loyalty to a group is a commitment about which we should therefore be delighted. In evangelism with children, Westerhoff would see us offering the opportunity to a child to become affiliated to a different structure in the church or group.

How much of this is linked with the teaching/learning situation and how much with personal experience which is itself linked with emotional maturity is debatable. The psychologists' opinions vary as to whether all this is directly linked with our chronological age or not.

Westerhoff would see this progression:

Experienced > Affiliative > Searching > Owned Faith

The sequence is always linked with chronological age.

James Fowler would see the process going on at different times in different people. For him it is more closely connected to the contents of a person's faith than to the age of the person. Conversion, he says, is a time when the contents of a person's faith are changed and this can happen at any time. At other times a development of faith is undergone by an experience which catapults someone from one stage of faith to another but without changing the content of the faith. It is not therefore conversion although it will intensify the faith and give new direction and sometimes dramatic change to that person's life.

For those reaching out to children in long-term nurture and evangelism, it is important to decide that each stage of this development of faith, where it is appropriate for the people concerned, is acceptable to the Creator God. In Bible terms God sees their inner state, their knowledge and understanding, and their response. In faith development terms we probably look for the best of both worlds of Fowler and Westerhoff. We want children to respond in a true child's way but to a true personal God.

Suppose that, as other research by Fowler has shown, the developmental pattern of faith continues at a pace which is directly affected by relationships and teaching – the community culture around that life. In that case, our position as leaders of children is extremely significant and our role as evangelists is justified. The problem in faith development is that we presume that all *development* is *growth* of faith – whereas it can be decline. This may be caused by lack of good Bible teaching, poor and misleading Christian models, as well as by hearing and rejecting the gospel. In this way, our teaching to those from churched families which we may see as nurture, is actually evangelism because it is to those inside the church who may be gradually growing away.

2.6 What about baptism?

The children of the ancient people of God were considered to be included in the Covenant God had made with all his people. The children of Christian people are seen to be in the Kingdom of God unless at some stage in life they specifically opt out. Obviously this faith will have times of personal commitment and stages of growing understanding as in any other person's life. The arrival of a new baby in a Christian home is the extension of the Kingdom of God just as the arrival of a baby to the Israelites was the means of increasing the people of God then.

This is expressed by the majority of Christians worldwide through the baptism of children when babies, with the minority preferring a form of dedication. When we bring a child to baptism as the community of God's people we:
1. recognize the Covenant which God has initiated.
2. commit ourselves to cherish the spiritual life of the family, which is the child's spiritual contact.
3. invite the Holy Spirit of God to work in this, his child, and therefore we commit ourselves to look with excitement and expectancy for the evidence of the growing life of the Spirit in that life.

In thinking about children in this way the Bible leads us to think about a two-layer basis for dealing with children and evangelism:

- God sees children in the context of their family. When children are born into a Christian home God sees them as being under the umbrella of their parents' faith – unless at some time they reject that faith.
- God sees children as individuals. He wants them to know and love him because they choose to. He looks for that personal response and commitment from them as he does from their parents and expects it to grow with their experience of him and their knowledge of his Word. All the promises – and demands – which are made for God's people are made for them.

2.7 What do children need to understand about the gospel?
Ideally, for children to understand salvation sufficiently to respond to God's love, they need to know:
- that God's intention was that Adam and Eve should not sin.
- that we caused the problem by our sin and caused an irreversible separation between God and the people he had made – because he is holy.

- that the separation and sin continue with anybody who is born on earth.
- that Jesus is the way God found to answer the problem and reverse it.
- that the way of Jesus is the only way in which people can be forgiven and receive the presence of the Holy Spirit into their lives.
- that each person needs to make that decision in order to come in/stay in the kingdom. In fact, this first step then sets a pattern of life for every day of their lives. It is what members of the kingdom of God do every day.

2.8 How might this be explained to children?

The teaching for children needs to cover this thought process and not suddenly leap into it part way along. If we dive in at the point where God provides Jesus as the answer to the problem, the children will not understand what the fuss is all about. If they do not understand the original problem, how can they be expected to value the salvation which was the answer to it?

One teaching programme we have used is:

Joseph (*Genesis chapters 37–46*) God does not look for perfect people to do his work because he knows we are all imperfect. God also knows that he can take the most imperfect people and change them as he forgives and then fills them with his Spirit.

Moses (*Exodus chapter 2–14*) God's plans are not just wishful thinking – they are certain to happen. Anyone who had decided not to obey God's plans would have been left behind in Egypt. God has a plan for the life of each of us. We can choose to be included in them.

Nehemiah (*Nehemiah chapters 1–4, 6, 12b*) God does impossible things magnificently. Things we see as being difficult are within the capabilities of our God. He sees with a totally different perspective from ours.

Elijah (1 Kings 18) God stands against wrong and says "That's wrong." Jesus Christ was the only human being God has ever looked at and said "That's right" at everything he did, said, thought and was.

Storm on the lake (Mark 4:35–41) The reason for that is that Jesus is God. The disciples realized this when they saw that Jesus not only behaved like God but had godly power over his creation.

Crucifixion (Mark 15) Even though Jesus is God, he chose to die. He knew that this was why the Father had sent him, because it was the only way for people to come to God through the barrier of wrong lives – sin.

None of this is easy stuff to teach to anyone. But if you want to check your understanding of a subject, try talking to a six-year-old about it. Then you'll know whether you *really* understand or are just hiding behind jargon and relying on the listener's prior knowledge of it.

As soon as I start to explain biblical truth to a group of children, I am left in no doubt in my own mind as to whether I understand what I am talking about. Explaining truth to children requires something from me which strips the jargon and side-issues from my mind. I am left with what I *really know* – and so are they. In talking the gospel to children, we are facing the gospel ourselves. If I cannot explain a biblical truth to an adult or out loud to myself, it would be disastrous to try to do so to a child.

Perhaps one of the reasons why presenting the gospel to children features so little in our church programmes is that those who would seem the natural people to do it are ill-equipped. They are often not affirmed in the work they are doing with churched children and therefore do not feel motivated to reach further afield to the unchurched. We will be looking further at this situation in Chapter 6, but the situation is often not a healthy one.

Vital questions to ask about the state of children's affairs in your church:
- How much regular training does your children's team have?
- On the whole, is their experience most likely to have been gained with churched or unchurched children?
- How much of their regular training is specifically for their contact with the unchurched children?
- Are we expecting them to cope without training in explaining the gospel to children who have no Christian vocabulary and understanding?

Think for a moment what regular contact with under-tens demands from an adult. It demands familiarity with the world of a child in the West at the end of the twentieth century. It will be at least a few years since those leaders were part of that world and it changes radically even in five years. This is quite apart from the general demands of regular contact with the under-tens like a lively sense of humour, a biblical understanding, a simple but profound vocabulary, an infinite store of patience, good ideas and tact with parents. In return, we often get very little feed-back from the children for our encouragement.

In spite of this, money for training of children's leaders is usually low down on the list of priorities for a church. Leaders are often given the impression that, not only is what they are doing going unnoticed by the church, but the church is prepared to put anyone who can walk and talk in leadership responsibility beside them. Children's leaders who are gifted and successful are frequently removed to answer apparently higher and more pressing needs like adult Home Groups.

If we are serious about children – and especially about evangelism – this attitude will not do. I was trained for three years before my profession let me loose in its primary schools and even then I was required to complete a year of closely supervised classroom experience before being a fully-fledged member of the teaching profession. Yet I was teaching the fairly simple material of letter recognition and basic number, physical and social skills.

But the education we are giving in our children's groups is teaching the Word of God. We are teaching truth without which God has said it is impossible to please him. We are modelling the way in which this truth changes people's lives, the way in which God forgives people and the Holy Spirit of God breathes his own personality into everyday lives. Is that important or not? Never mind the investment for our church's future – what about the "now" of their lives as children of a mighty, powerful, holy Creator? Does it matter how we do that teaching? The only way for the necessary change to come to our churches is when we can answer a resounding "Yes" to this question. We will then find out what is involved in teaching the Bible to children.

Be warned!
My experience is that it takes twice as long to prepare Bible teaching for children as a sermon for any other service. It takes the same biblical preparation, but needs a similar length of time preparing the vocabulary, analogies and visual presentation. Why is it so time-consuming? I talk as an adult to adults and therefore *to some extent* speak their language wherever I am. However, I am never a child and therefore the demanding effort to speak and communicate clearly will always be there. It is now well over twenty years since I left college and I have spent all that time working with children or bringing up my own, yet I still find this gargantuan effort is needed if I am going to explain the truth clearly.

Many of our regular leaders will need help to think through the chapters in Part 2. They will need to break out of the thinking pattern which has grown from the old "Sunday School" model. As they learn to plan specifically for evangelism they will find that Chapters 5–8 try to blow the dust off

our methods of communication with children. I want us to
start from the ideal and work towards reality rather than
start with the predictable and mundane – and stay there. We
are not setting our agenda around the way we find most
satisfying to teach and communicate. We are setting about
finding the way in which children are stimulated and relaxed
enough to listen, learn and remember.

We may feel relaxed:
- because someone is making us laugh
- because we feel we belong and have a right to be
  there
- because we like and are confident with the people
  around us.

Usually it is a combination of those factors.

It is interesting that for many people in our culture
this would make the local pub the ideal venue for education.

Our theology will affect the way we present Bible teaching
and apply it, as well as the way we choose our programme.
If our starting point is that everything we say and do is vitally
important and significant for each child because of the way
God views the child, then our presentation will reflect this.

We will make sure that what we say and the way we say
it are clear. This affects our choice of vocabulary. It also
means we teach only one point in a session. Children's sessions so often point in several directions. This is confusing.
Children will only remember one thing clearly anyway – this
is true of adults too – so why not make sure they remember
the one truth which is vital for that session? The multi-point
session may all link together but rather than strengthen the
learning experience, it actually weakens it.

Make it clear that you are not a detached know-it-all but are sharing your faith and understanding as you go on learning too.

Use Bible material to teach biblical points.

If you use other material make it very clear to the children that this is not from the Bible – and it should still make biblical points.

Make sure your main point is teaching what the Bible teaches.

Make sure everything in the session underlines that one point.

Expect God to bring it home to the understanding of the children.

Make sure the children know how to communicate their reaction to you.

2.9 Abrupt turn-about or steady change?

When adults are talking about their growth of faith, they usually talk about little changes which have happened regularly over a long period of time rather than a big turning point. The big turning point which we call conversion is not an isolated, significant incident. The turning to God of his creation is often better described on a curve rather than an abrupt turn. That is not to undervalue conversion – quite the opposite.

Conversion is a marker which we put down in our growth of faith and godliness. For us to consider it the only such marker means we will not look to grow beyond that point. There should be many such markers. When children put down that marker, we should recognize that many small steps of growth of faith have already taken place. We need to make sure that they do not see conversion as "having arrived" but as a very significant agreement which they have made with God. He has been working in their lives all this time and now they have recognized it. They will need to go on recognizing this every day for the rest of their lives.

2.10 What can we expect as a reasonable response from a child?

Often people who are teaching the gospel to children are so concerned not to put pressure on children to respond that they give them no opportunity to respond at all. James Thurber said quite rightly, "You might as well fall flat on your face as lean over too far backwards." We need to inform children about what an appropriate response is, even if some of them are not ready yet to make such a response.

So how can they respond?
You might choose to invite them to come to a workshop or club session which is just for:
- children with questions
- children who want to know more about belonging to the kingdom of God
- children who know Jesus and want to talk to you about following him more closely

Whatever the arrangements try to make sure that:
- they can be reasonably undisturbed
- there is no pressure for them to produce a certain response
- when they have found out the answers to the questions they came with, they are free to go

---

Accept, above all, that it is always difficult to gauge what God is doing in the lives of others, especially children. God does so much of his work in secret and we are asked to be faithful, and obedient, but not nosey. As we ask God to renew our eyes we will see more and more of what he is doing – but never all.

At each point where you take stock of evangelistic outreach:
- there will be children who have reached out in faith to God through Jesus for the first time;
- there will be others who have had a long but secret faith

who will have spoken to a friend about Jesus for the first time;
• there will be children who have always had a relationship with God but now find their faith has understanding and ownership.

Some of this we will see and we can then celebrate with those who celebrate. But we need always to be aware that we see only a little and one day we will be staggered by what God has achieved. Be assured that God has worked wherever the gospel has been taught, and pray for that assurance for each child who has made an open response.

If you look back through this chapter you will find a mixture of theology and practical ideas. It is always dangerous to leave theology behind when we dive into practical arrangements. The theology must come with us as a continual point of reference. Who are we to decide that "the end justifies the means" in our evangelism when the Bible is there for us from the start?

◊ **Look back**
1. Can you know the facts of the gospel? Do you know the gospel from your own experience?
2 When was the last time you put your faith into words to someone with no knowledge of Christianity or the Bible?
3 How frequently do you give the Christian children you know the opportunity to put their faith into words, either to you or to their peer group?

◊ **Look forward**
We have seen the child in the setting of the Kingdom of God. Now we shall look at the same children again but this time in their secular setting. Unless we see them realistically in this setting our approach to them with the gospel and our attempts to nurture will come to nothing.

3

Real World

3.1 Encountering the real world

When I first came to live in Birmingham, I obtained a job teaching on "permanent supply". This meant that every three weeks I was moved to a different school. My role was to replace a member of staff who was attending a central course. For the first term this was in secondary education and the second was in primary. I was a primary teacher and the last time I had been in secondary school had been as a pupil. Suddenly after nearly twenty years I was teaching young people who were at least six years older than the children I had been trained to teach.

I was covering any subject taught by the absent member of staff – from Biology to German. I did not know the area, understand the accent or know much about the ethnic groups represented in my classes. I can remember saying in total exasperation to one lad who was at least a foot taller than me, "If I could reach to box your ears – I would." Mercifully, he had a good sense of humour and sat down to facilitate this. The incident ended with laughing.

Not all of the situations did though, and I was aware that the regular members of staff were struggling with the same issues – the huge need to understand the context of the people you are teaching, to realize that their culture, language, religion, age and philosophy make each one unique. I'd never seen people sitting in tears in a staff room before. Society had radically changed in a very few years.

3.2 How does society influence a child?

The child is in society. We all operate within it. The evangelism we are talking about can only take place in society. The response of children to the Gospel will depend partly on whether our communication is directly influenced by our knowledge of the society we are in – or whether we are unaware of the changes which have taken place since we were children ourselves.

One of the projects I undertook when I was at training college was a survey of the village in which my family lived at the time. The project was presented in the form of slides and a taped commentary. Now, twenty five years later, it is obviously dated. Not only do the equipment, type of film and standard of recording indicate that it was made so long ago, but the issues addressed by the project are not ones which are of any current interest. The photos of children and cars, the fashion of clothes and the method of farming are of a previous generation. Some of these things are more obvious than others. Some would simply be a feeling and impression from seeing the slides or hearing the commentary.

In that way, society is made up from a thousand details and it changes, often imperceptibly, as each year goes by. Some of these changes are spelt out for us as each season brings a new look in the fashion shows and car brochures. Others are less noticeable and, even after twenty years, it would be hard to label what they are – we just know when people are not reflecting that change when they communicate. It sounds and feels wrong.

Those subtle changes in communication are to do with:
- the way in which people speak
  - not just the vocabulary they use
- the way in which different groups relate to each other
  - groups of gender, age, race, politics
- the speed at which life moves
  - on the street and in business
- the emphasis of the time
  - on appearance, or health, or possessions, or education

When we communicate with children, it is important to remember that they are part of today's society. They have been born into today's society so they are not viewing it as we do – as part of a series. It is the only one they know. They have not experienced any other kind of society so they belong to it in a different way from us. Unless we recognize this we will become part of the group of evangelists who go on doing what they have done for years, in the way they have always done it, on the basis that "God has used it before, so why change?" We need to get to know our society – see it with our eyes open – so that what we use to contact the children of that society will be really appropriate for them. *We* need to be the ones to adapt, not the children.

When we are with people of our own kind – our religion, age, type, academic background, financial and professional position – we relate and communicate automatically with ease. As soon as we cross any one of those barriers we feel constraint. If this lack of ease is slight, we may simply avoid the subject which causes it. When the constraint is extreme, we need to find ways of understanding what is causing it and ways to bridge it.

When people go to work abroad, this need is obvious. I went to live in Ethiopia in my early twenties and I never forgot that the people around me were different from me, and neither did they. We ate different food and spoke a different language, we wore different clothes and we felt a similar curiosity about each other's way of life. Our communication was built on the understanding of how different we were rather than by ignoring that.

But this situation is often not recognized when we are in our own country. Perhaps we feel that other people should make the effort to bridge the gap rather than ourselves. Remember, this gap is not simply one of race but it exists between children and adults, churched and unchurched, professional and manual worker, female and male, wealthy and poor. If we want to communicate with someone deeply we cannot afford to avoid the unease. Instead we need to get to know that person's background. Unless we recognize this gap and work hard to get to know the context of the child we are reaching out to, we will give offence and we will cause dilemma and confusion for the child.

The only way to bridge the gap is to become familiar with their context – not to expect them to get used to ours. We need to know what their daily pattern of living is like, the sort of television programmes they regularly watch, the activities they choose in their free time, the sort of education they are receiving. If we are not prepared to do this then this book, and any like it, is a waste of time – we shall never be understood when we explain the gospel.

3.3 What influence does the family have on a child?

Finding out about children's daily pattern of living will high-light one remarkable institution within our society – the family. The strength of family feelings, both negative and positive, is a force to be reckoned with. When my two sons were small, they bickered with varying depth of feeling from when they woke in the morning until they went to bed at night. But if either of them was in trouble and under attack from someone outside, they closed ranks and became "the Frank boys".

Think of all the different sorts of family which may be represented in a group of children.
Their homes may be:
Christian, atheist, agnostic, academic, wealthy, poor.
Their homes may be places where the television is watched all the time
– or where people go out a lot to the theatre or to concerts.
They may be children whose every desire is met
– or those who are treated worse than the furniture.
Their parents may not care about the future of their children
– or they may have high aspirations for them.
The children may have attended playgroup or nursery school

– or they may have been looked after by an elderly relative.
They may have been used to using creative materials from babyhood
– or may not have touched dough or paint until they went to school.

Obviously most of the families represented by children we meet for evangelism are more likely to be somewhere in the middle rather than at the two extremes, but the range is amazing. Because of the strength of the family factor, in both churched or unchurched, it can be very difficult to get to know a family well. You may be allowed inside it, you may even on occasions feel an *ad hoc* member of it, but only in so far as that family allows you to be. This means that any evangelism in which we are involved will be affected by the family – both in terms of what the children are encouraged to do and in the up-bringing which will affect everything the child hears.

▷ We should welcome parents who check on the arrangements we make for their children. Often it is only the people of other faiths who stay to find out what we are teaching. We should encourage Christian adults to check us out. After all, the responsibility for these children is theirs and it is a responsibility given to them by God.

The range of families needs to be in our minds when we are in evangelism because often we jump to the wrong conclusions. If, for example, we assume that the children of Christian homes will be the most well cared for of all – we may be surprised. If we assume that the parents of Christian homes will be the most likely to check out what we are teaching their children – we may have a shock.

3.4 What influence does a Christian family have on a child?
Whatever the standard of parenting, a Christian family is
special. It will provide a framework for evangelism and is
evangelistic in itself. But it would be misleading to suppose
that the background of a Christian family will guarantee
success when it comes to evangelism, making the steady
growth of faith a foregone conclusion.

Church families can be divided into four types:
- Families who have a silent faith.
- Families with a hypocritical faith.
- Families with an open faith.
- Families who make no difference between the faith
  of a child and that of an adult.

Each of these will have a totally different effect on the
child and therefore on our evangelism. We need to be
aware of this huge range and not lump them all together
as Christian families.

- *There are families who have a silent faith.*
They go to church together and will have a certain agreed
set of Christian ethics around which the whole family operates but this will never be openly discussed in any way.
Often the thinking in these families can be quite muddled.
In the home where I grew up, I was never sure whether I
was required to do something because we were Christian
people and the Bible said so, or whether this was something
which "nice families" did, or whether it had something to
do with the politics of my parents – since these carried with
them the same sort of aura.

Children in these families grow up with an increasing list
of questions because, on the whole, they are being shown
what to do and be, but never given the reason why. My
mind has always felt like a tumbling heap of questions on
most subjects and I used to wonder what the adults around
me would do if they saw inside my mind and knew those

questions. Since none of them was expressed the questions did not promote my young faith at all.

Sometimes the family silence is carried over by its members into other relationships. Children will find it very difficult to break out in order to talk to a leader about their faith or to pray in a group of children – even when their friends do. They would not have the vocabulary and range of expression to put their knowledge and faith into words. It will just sound jargon when they do. Sometimes the experience of going on a Christian holiday or attending a Christian club will give them the release they need to speak out what they think and feel. This will usually not have a knock-on effect into the family. Even though I became more and more confident and articulate in speaking about my faith as I went through school and college, I never found any ease of communication about matters of faith with my Christian parents.

We need to be sensitive to the difficulties such a child is facing in communication with us and their peer group members. Their biggest difficulty will be in communicating back to their family the spiritual growth they have experienced. We will need to make sure that we do not make them feel guilty about this with pressure about "confessing with their mouth". After all, the situation at home is not of their making and they do not have, as a child, the power to break through that silence.

● *There are families who have a hypocritical faith.*
This is, of course, a dangerous condemnation to make unless I want the finger pointed back at me. I am talking here though about the dilemma Christian children experience when they hear one set of rules or slogans from their parents in public but know that a totally different set apply at home. I remember experiencing this at first hand when a close friend was being beaten up by her husband – both members of a local church. Their children presented an air of perpetual confusion and dilemma. That is an extreme case. Yet many children are told not to steal, but know that their parents will supply certain stationery needs from work; know that

they should not lie, but hear half-truths being told by their parents in their social lives.

Obviously the children from these homes will behave in a similar way themselves. We may feel when we are talking to them that they are offering conversation which is appropriate for the situation rather than really being themselves. Their reaction to us is likely to be wary – after all, how do they know that *we* are telling the truth and being real with them? How do they know that when God says something it *is* truth and not simply something which he has manufactured for the occasion to keep them temporarily comfortable? We will need to accept any response they make to our evangelism on the basis that this is their background and that the response – whatever that is – may be simply a superficial one which they consider appropriate.

● *There are families who have an open faith.*
This sounds the perfect answer but can feel just as full of danger. By "an open faith" I mean one in which not only is the parent free to explain to the child areas of faith and belief, but the child and parent grow increasingly able to share areas of questions and difficulty. This is never easy to maintain. Some member of the family may feel pressured to respond in a certain way because nothing is private. One child may be very open and articulate causing another sibling to withdraw.

A friend of ours used to grow carrots. Periodically, he would pull up a few to see how they were progressing and then stick them back in the ground to continue growing. Naturally, at the harvest, it was easy to see the stunted growth of the ones which had been pulled in and out of the ground. The family with the open faith may sound ideal but it can produce just such a harvest.

Children from the family with the open faith may therefore not be as articulate as you expect them to be in small groups – they are thankful for the opportunity to be private. They may thoroughly enjoy taking the spectator role for a change. These children are often the ones who will suddenly, at the end of the event when a leader has labelled them as uninterested, come out with a remark or observation which stuns everyone with its accuracy and sharp discernment.

● *There are families who make no difference between the faith of an adult and the faith of a child.*
Many Christian adults think that a person cannot have a real faith in God until they are adult. Others think of adults and children as being on the same footing when it comes to Christian growth and faith. The attitudes expressed in the home about the child's faith will have a noticeable influence on them, both in evangelism and nurture.

Children from a family which encourages them to believe for themselves will display a confidence in faith which will be quite different, in my observation, from other children. They are more likely to consider their opinions and knowledge and experience worth sharing both with you and with their friends. They will know, far beyond your telling them, that they are special to God. They will be growing up in the sure knowledge of his delight in all their progress and development.

The family is the most significant influence in the life of any child. It casts a long shadow and its effect can be seen much later in life in the roles of parents and grandparents. Everything is affected by the way in which people are parented themselves. Our evangelism should be built on a thorough knowledge of the different ways in which the influence of parents will be demonstrated in the area where we are evangelizing.

3.5 What part do fashion and culture play?
Fashion changes, and not just in clothes. There is a changing fashion in music and the other arts too – poetry, drama, colours, television themes, school equipment, school uniform. The fashion wheel turns continually.

> **Culture and fashion overlap, but:**
> *Fashion* tends to be something which is quickly replaced by the next layer of experience.
> *Culture* is that which has built up over generations of experience and is added to by each layer of experience.

The idea of the evangelist following the whole course of that wheel would, of course, be ridiculous; it would be another full-time job. However, the idea of the evangelist being clueless about any of the current trends is equally ridiculous. It is impossible to communicate into a world about which one has no knowledge. It would mean that all the illustrations and links belonged to another society. It would be like someone going to preach the gospel in another country before going through an orientation course or living in the country for any length of time – the mistakes made would be horrendous.

One children's leader was heard teasing a child for her "dirty hands". She was from a culture with a tradition of colouring the palms of the hands as decoration for a wedding or special feast. There were many children from that ethnic group in the area. The leader needed to know some of these basic facts before engaging in evangelism there. Other leaders had to step in and put the situation right before that child felt relaxed and at ease.

3.6 What attitudes has school encouraged in the child?

School, of course, makes up a large proportion of the society in which the child lives – in fact it is probably the main outside influence on the life of any child under ten. Each day the child will spend between six and seven hours being moulded by the atmosphere and philosophy of this establishment. No wonder when a child quotes at home anyone of authority on any subject, that person is likely to be connected with school. The person quoted may be a member of the teaching staff, the gardener, a "dinner lady" or the daddy of a schoolfriend – their position is immaterial, their connection with school gives them credence.

The easiest way for the Budding Children's Evangelist (the BCE) to feel the effect of this influence is to make an extended visit to the local school at least once in a school year. It is easy to forget the power of the peer group and to stop making allowances for it in evangelism if we are never in a situation where children are in the majority and on their own territory. A day in school, especially if it is a school which caters for the children in your area, will help to keep this influence in your mind as you prepare for evangelism.

If certain aspects of the life of your local school are good, you are likely to find your outreach to children very enjoyable. If there are parts of the life of the school which are not so encouraging because of, say, a rough catchment area or poor premises, you may well have some problems in your evangelism. But at least the school visit will have given you some warning about these in advance.

> ▷ **If the school** gives easy access to parents at any time of the school day, then you can expect parents to be prepared to come onto your church premises easily and to be involved in the ways you suggest.
>
> ▷ **If the school** discourages parents from appearing on the school premises except by appointment, you may well find you have to work hard as a team to make contact with the parents, to invite them over the doorstep when they bring children, to insist that they collect the child from a certain part of the building at the end of the event.
>
> ▷ **If the general attitude** towards children in the school is to treat what they say as of great interest, you will find not only that they enter into conversation with leaders easily, but that they will be quite free with questions and comments on the Bible material you present.
>
> ▷ **If the school** is more concerned that the children listen to the staff – and this often has considerable

emphasis in areas where discipline is a problem – there is likely to be little specific comment from the children on the Bible material, but this will not necessarily mean that they have not been listening or understanding.

It's also worth finding out details about the curriculum in the school before an evangelistic event. From this you will know what sort of activities the children will be interested in for workshops, and you will know also to what activities you can expect the children to contribute.

For example, if the school has a lively attitude towards drama and music but has little space for sport, you can expect quite a high level of contribution towards music and drama, but any sport workshops would probably be especially popular. The best way to find all this out is by the informal method of spending time with families from the church who have children at the school. Children will usually chat about school without reserve and will probably give you all the information you need in a short space of time.

3.7 How has any earlier experience of church life affected the child?

The children you are praying for may never have had experience of church life. On the other hand you may be reaching out to groups of children which include those with regular experience of church.

We are the church, and anything we say in evangelism will be coloured in the child's mind by any previous experience of church however shallow and unrepresentative that has been. The unchurched child will have experienced school visits, parade services, family weddings, all of which leave impressions of church.

These will range from an awareness that church buildings are different from others – places where you cannot see out – to the fact that people behave differently – they do not sit close together as they do in a home or school. When we move into evangelism with children, the BCE needs to bear this in mind because it will affect the way in which children respond to invitations to come and also to their expectations when they do attend.

3.8 How has your experience of church affected you?
It is not simply the children to whom we are explaining the gospel who will be affected by their previous experience. The evangelists for your event, both adults and children, are members of your church. What goes on in your church will have made them the sort of people they are and will have contributed hugely to the way they are thinking about evangelism anyway. It is also important to recognize that when you welcome them into the Kingdom of God, you welcome them into the church. It is important to look at your church realistically *before* your event rather than in horror or panic *afterwards*.

Ask yourself these questions about your church:
- Do all the age-groups meet together for every activity within the life of the church?
- Are all the age-groups kept totally separate in every activity?
- How closely does the *teaching* of the church tie up with the *life* of the church members?
- Is it easy for children to join a group of their own age if their parents do not attend church?
- Is there an easy transitionary period between the different age-groups of the church – say between primary and secondary age?
- Do the members of the children's groups find their groups attractive enough to want to invite other children to join?

Here are some of the reasons why these questions need to be answered:

● *Is it All-Age Everything?*
It can be very difficult for children who are making the transition from a specialist group to come straight into an all-age event, especially in a large church. To the newcomer, it appears that everyone in a Family Service is part of a family unit. It is almost impossible to expect primary age children to feel part of this, unless their parents have agreed to accompany them or a leader from their original specialist group substitutes as parents.

The newcomers may also find the change in teaching approach very daunting. They will probably be accustomed to a group where all the Bible teaching has been geared to them. Now suddenly they find that belonging to the church is not simply belonging to Jesus but joining in an activity where they do not understand everything.

The best way for newcomers to feel there is a place for them in the All-Age set-up is if each church family is asked to adopt an unchurched newcomer. The church family can approach the parents with an invitation, they can collect the child who will then sit with them, and they can be prepared to chat about what has happened in the service with the child on the way home.

Be warned – you will need to be prepared for a long-term commitment.

● *Is it Separate Everything?*
This is very much simpler for the initial invitation and arrangements. You are inviting children to a group which operates just for their age-group and the name of the group will usually make this clear. However, the drawback of this introduction to church life is that these children only see adults in the teaching role. For them to understand what Jesus meant by the church, they need not only to see their leaders as part of the whole church but to be given some understanding of their own position in that church too. Some of this may need to be explained from the beginning – otherwise belonging to Jesus will be the same as joining Explorers or Sunday School.

Another problem is that it can be harder to invite parents

and the rest of the family to church if on entry to the building each member is syphoned off to different rooms. How will the caring unchurched parent be able to check what is going on in their children's rooms if they are expected to stay in the adult room? We become so used to the arrangements made in our churches that we often do not realize how strange these seem to a newcomer.

● *Are the teaching and the life of the church compatible?*
A child is rarely fooled by hypocrisy. If the group of people who worship in a church are seen to be saying one thing and doing another, the child will quickly pick this up. The reaction of the child will either be to learn that this is the particular pattern of behaviour which is necessary for membership of the church, or else to discard it. Hypocrisy will either breed more hypocrisy – or contempt.

Look at the churched children you have. How have they reacted to church life? Are they wary of parents and adult friends who are not dependable in what they do and say – or is there real trust and openness?

● *Attractive groups – children ready to reach their peer group?*
The last three points go together. If the groups in the church are easy to belong to and fun to be at; if they operate at a time when children can enjoy them and not at a time when the children feel they are being "got out of the way"; if the sense of belonging to the groups is good and one of worshipping and learning together with a small group of adults – then children will want to invite their friends.

Their friends will already know about the groups anyway because the members will have talked at school about the good things they have enjoyed at church. If the groups are good, it will not simply be the exciting activities which will be talked about at school but some of the talk will be about spiritual things too – the two will not be seen as separate by the members of the group. This means that you will already have children who are naturally involved in evangelism. When you talk about going on learning to live God's way, many children will know that the church is the place to do that.

3.9 What is happening in your area?
The area where you live will have distinctive features.

Think about your area:
- What are the main group divides which are notice-able there (for example, age, race, economic)?
- With which of these does the church mainly deal?
- Which of these groups offers the fewest barriers to communication with the church?
- Which of these groups offers the biggest barriers to communication with the church?
- Are there obvious ways to find out about these barriers?
- Which members of your leadership team are most able to communicate with the groups which are hardest to reach?

Once you are concerned to break through these barriers, ways can be found. The biggest barrier of all is if the church shrugs its shoulders and says "God will cope". Praise God that this is true, but this does not justify our ignorance. Equally we will be in difficulties if we assume other churches in the area are doing the job for us or if we ignore what they are doing and decide to cover the same ground – properly. We have a responsibility to find out what is going on in our area among its groups and to reach out accordingly – otherwise all our words will fall on deaf ears. All our evangelism will achieve is to salve our consciences. We've told them but they have not heard.

3.10 What is the national church doing about the situation?
The national church is very aware that the teaching and explanation of the gospel to children has declined to a worry-ing level. A report for the General Synod of the Church of

England aimed to spread this message through the whole of the national church by having representatives of all the main denominations on the working party.

The report says:
Please do not ignore the problem any longer.
Please do not leave the situation in the hands of the few unresourced, exhausted children's evangelists.
Please read, look and talk about the situation and its potential in your area.
Please then stand up and move into action.

The report tries to break through the mystique surrounding evangelism – that it is only for certain people at certain times. It quotes the Rev Dr John Stott in *Christian Mission in the Modern World* where he says: "To evangelize, in the New Testament usage, does not mean to win converts as it usually does when we use the word. Evangelism is the announcement of the good news, irrespective of the results." The Bible makes it clear that our responsibility as Christians is to proclaim the Good News.

- Romans 10:14 asks: "How can they call on the one they have not believed in? And how can they believe in the one of whom they have not heard? And how can they hear without someone preaching to them?"
- John 4:37 describes Jesus warning his disciples that those who sow are often not the ones who reap. We may never see the results.
- 2 Thessalonians 3.1 encourages us to pray, and to galvanize the church to pray, for the message to be heard and received.

Too many evangelists have done the church the dis-service of head-counting results – and announcing their score. Presumably this is to convince their supporters that they are worth supporting. Evangelism is the announcing of the good news clearly, in a way in which the audience can understand – after that the evangelist's job is done. The Synod report aims to move the church into being able and willing to announce the good news. And if we decide not to do that, then we must answer the question, what is a church for?

The recommendations included in the report focus on spiritual aspects which need reform like prayer, and also on the practical side of evangelism like money; it offers an audit in which the parish can assess its needs and its resources. The report encourages churches to steer their congregations towards involvement in schools, both with supply of Christian teachers and also at a daily, informal level. It looks at the way in which the situation in theological colleges could be improved in order to prepare men and women for their work with children, both in schools and in the churches. It encourages co-operation between people who are working with children, in the church, in schools and in society as a whole.

Certainly, the national church now has no excuse for not understanding the need for teaching the Gospel to children. The present situation has been spelt out clearly and directions forward have been suggested in this report.

◊ **Looking back**
- How much do you know about the context of the children you are reaching out to?
- When did you last spend time with children in their family setting or in the context of their school?
- Have you taken a realistic look at the way in which your experience of church has influenced your evangelism – and will welcome new arrivals?

◊ **Looking forward**
Often when we are brave enough to look carefully at the real world we can start to despair. The good news is that we have been sent to evangelize by a real and powerful God who is able to explain the Gospel and to change the hearts and minds of people as they hear. The next chapter will look at the ways in which we can see him work.

4

Real God

Peter has a secret friend called Andrew. He thinks that having a brother would be a really good idea. Unfortunately, his parents do not share this view of things, so he has ended up with a secret friend instead. In fact, Peter is finding the secret friend a really good idea because Andrew is sometimes older than Peter so he can be helpful and protective; sometimes Peter is the elder one and can tell him what he has done, expecting admiration; Andrew never goes away to someone else because no one else knows about him. Andrew is the person Peter talks to all the time, when he cannot find something or he is feeling lonely or he just needs someone to shout at. Andrew is always the same and always there.

Peter is not the only eight-year-old to have a secret, silent, imaginary companion – many children do.

The imagination, to children, is part and parcel of their world. That is why they find it difficult to know the difference between something which really happened and something which is pretend – between truth and fiction. It is only as they grow up slowly through the years of adolescence that the distinction becomes clear. So imaginary and real people, events of history and those of folklore, things they have done and things they would like to do, all have the same significance.

4.1 How do adults relate to the different persons of the Trinity?

This truth about children makes the argument we have in the church about the Trinity very odd. It is argued that it will be at different stages of my life that I will relate to Jesus as my forgiving friend, or God as my holy Creator, or the

Holy Spirit as my powerful companion. People feel concerned about introducing the persons of the Trinity at the "wrong time". They worry about how children will imagine the Holy Spirit when they cannot see him, or that they might picture God as an elderly grey-haired man. They say that Jesus is the only member of the Trinity to whom a child can relate because they can imagine how he really was.

Can children really imagine Jesus how he really was? I can't. I can *try* to imagine Jesus by reading the Gospels and I can look at people in the Middle East and imagine what his colouring and build might have been. But that is pulling into play all sorts of information which I have gathered as an adult. We have already said that the world of the child is not just a seen world.

Delve into your imagination for a moment:
- What did Jesus look like when he was on earth?
- What does Jesus look like now?
- What do you imagine when you talk to God?
- Which person of the Trinity do you usually address when you pray?
- Do you ever pray to the Holy Spirit?
- What picture do you have in your mind when you talk to the Holy Spirit?
- When you arrive in heaven and you meet God, which of the three persons you have imagined are you expecting to see?

It seems that we all find it easier, when we introduce God to children, to introduce the person of the Trinity with whom we are most comfortable. This is only logical. If I usually pray to Jesus, then it is likely that I will be most comfortable with the "image" of Jesus and will therefore tend to introduce him to the children in my home or my group. This means that I will usually tell stories of Jesus, I will always address my prayers in the group to Jesus and will encourage the children to do the same by the way I introduce prayer time.

This is at best unfortunate – because the Trinity is an important doctrine. The Trinity is not there in order to cater for our different preferences when dealing with a God whom we cannot see. We need to give our children the opportunity to communicate with all three persons of the Trinity.

My father always shook his head over my imagination and said things like: "One day, your imagination will get you into trouble." Although as prophecy this lacked a certain punch, it was probably dead right over the years since. As a child, everything came into my mind automatically in a pictorial form. So, for example, numbers went in a zig-zagging ladder; new words had a sound-shape when I *heard* them which meant I often did not recognize them in a book if they had a different written shape; I retain strong visual memories of people I meet though I rarely remember names or where I met them. Not surprisingly, I used my imagination on God, too.

- I imagined God the Father sitting with the newspaper so that he could be with me all the time – after all, he would have to do something to pass the time when I wasn't talking to him.
- I imagined Jesus only as arms/hands which helped/ comforted/ punished/ lifted me up to see God (always a problem when you are small) and, for some reason which I cannot remember, conducted the choirs of angels. In fact I used to think how well the angels had apparently done on Christmas Eve, with their usual conductor lying in a manger.
- I always imagined the Holy Spirit as beautiful perfume, though I do not know the origin of that thought.

The Trinity is three persons – each and all of the Trinity is God. The Bible teaches the Trinity as a fundamental wonder of the Godhead and we need to respond to this rather than use it as a "Pick and Mix" opportunity. If we don't, quite apart from the spiritual poverty this will produce in our own lives, it will also produce patchy teaching in our leadership.

It's easy to teach a child:
- God made you.
- God made you so he delights in you.
- God delights in you so he found a way to enjoy your company.
- The way is Jesus.
- Jesus was kind, good, truthful – a good friend to have.
- Jesus died but death could not keep hold of him.
- Jesus is still alive.
- Jesus is still a good friend to have.

Unfortunately, in introducing God to children we have traditionally concentrated on God the Son. After all, there are so many "real stories" about Jesus and it is so much easier to introduce someone who did and said certain things and behaved in a certain way. This has been good and is even more important now that most children grow up without hearing the events of the Gospels at all. It is good – but it is not all that children need to learn about God.

Leaders introducing God to children have tended to bring in God the Father much later. Many of them have done this tentatively, either because they have had experience of bad father models themselves or because they are afraid the children have. This is unfortunate, since it is the people and children who have previously met a bad father model who most need to meet our heavenly Father. He is the God who made them, and who then bought them back, although they are already his. Surely we do not need to be wary in introducing a God who "loved the world so much that he gave".

In whatever way leaders have introduced the Father and the Son, it is certainly the Holy Spirit who has been left to one side. Most adults have found him the difficult person of the Trinity to understand themselves so they feel that children can certainly not cope with him. His coming to the disciples is described in terms of confusion – rushing mighty wind, strange tongues, people thrown into prison again and again for foolish determination to preach. By contrast, the coming of Jesus can conjure up a cuddly bundle who looked like any other baby and about whose birth glitter and legend can freely flow. If we feel like this we need to recognize that we are not teaching the coming of Jesus correctly, because the ugliness and starkness of the cross were there in Bethlehem. It certainly gives us no licence for leaving out the introduction of the Holy Spirit to children.

The Holy Spirit is the "How" of all that truth. We are going to look in some detail now at who he is and what he does not because he is more important than the other persons of the Trinity, but because he is the person who is most incorrectly taught in our approach to children. The Holy Spirit brings the assurance of salvation. So although we may find it easier to teach about the Father, Creator God and the Saviour Son who was a friend of sinners, we must teach the Holy Spirit too.

4.2 What is the work of the Holy Spirit?

We need not feel concerned that we cannot give the children a definite description of the Holy Spirit. We need first to examine what the Bible teaches about him, while being aware of our own attitudes, assumptions and imagination. These are bound to be reflected in the way we introduce God to children and the way we react to his presence in their lives.

> **Even in one of Paul's letters, the work of the Holy Spirit is described as varied and powerful:**
> - He demonstrates God's power alongside preaching (1 Corinthians 2:4).
> - He comes to bring us understanding (1 Corinthians 2:9–12).
> - He gives us spiritual words to speak spiritual truths (1 Corinthians 2:13).

- He comes to give discernment, and frees us from the judgement of people (1 Corinthians 2:15).
- He makes us into God's temple by living in us (1 Corinthians 3:16, 6:19).
- He washes, sanctifies, justifies us (1 Corinthians 6:11).
- He directs all honour and praise to Jesus (1 Corinthians 12:3).
- He gives all spiritual gifts (1 Corinthians 12:4).
- He determines the distribution of gifts (1 Corinthians 12:11).
- He brings acceptance of that gift (faith) (1 Corinthians 12:9).

The work of the Holy Spirit is so varied and the way in which he introduces the work of God in a community is often so individual. He seems to be very accommodating in the way he works. He often seems to work within our own expectations of him. He is not out to shock and confuse. This is not to say that he does not surprise – far from it. But he does seem to work in churches and groups in the way in which the group expects.

This is often what causes the arguments. Each group thinks their theories about the Holy Spirit are proved because "that is the way God is working in our group". We therefore discard what is happening in other groups as being "too over the top" and therefore of the devil, or of being "inhibited" and therefore quenching the Spirit. Probably neither is true. God is doing his work in a way with which that group can cope.

4.3 Why is the Holy Spirit the most difficult person to teach to children?

The reason we find ourselves wary of the Holy Spirit is often a commendable one – we want to be sure that this is God and not our imaginations at work. When we are with children we feel that concern even more. It is so easy for anyone with communication skills and training to provoke and manipulate children to exhibit spiritual manifestations, especially in a large group. This is why many people hardly seem to expect God to work in individual lives of children at all. They leave to one side the teaching about spiritual gifts because of the problems it presents. They stick to teaching about "not telling lies" and "obeying parents" – both quite valid, of course, but only part of the truth. The trouble is that when we stick to safe areas we find we all have different areas which we would call "unsafe".

One of our reservations may be because we *do* believe what we are teaching. In that case, we may be worried that God may give children gifts and evidences of his presences which we will envy. Be prepared – he probably will. God knows how to give good gifts to his children and there will be times when you will see what he is doing in a child and be aware of a deep longing to be a child again. There are times when you may be dealing with a child from an unchurched background who has such an uncluttered approach to God that everything seems fresh and obvious. You may find yourself watching this with longing and envy.

Be glad that you are working with children who are responding like this. As you worship with them, teach them, answer their questions and live out your Christian life next to theirs, you are having what the Bible calls "fellowship" with them. That is a wonderful situation to be in. Maybe they will have gifts which you would love to have, but this need not inhibit you or even be alarming. God gives the gifts, and he grows the fruit in our lives. He will be blessing your life through the children you are leading – that is *not* a humiliating experience.

4.4 How do adults recognize the work of God in their lives?

The trouble is that when we think about the work of the Holy Spirit, we tend to talk solely in terms of Bible teaching and lists. However that Bible teaching will direct us to know the truth from experience as well as fact.

The first is the most important. The second must not be ignored.

If experience is valid they will both be saying the same.

Certainly when we come to look at what the Holy Spirit can do – and is likely to do – in his work with children, we need to bear both in mind. We are likely to recognize God's work in children only if we know what the Bible teaches about the way he works and we can recognize God's work in us.

These are some of the ways in which I recognize the work of the Holy Spirit in my life:

- When I realize that I really want to see that evidence. If I *want* to see God working, then the Holy Spirit *is* working. My natural desire is *away* from God but the Holy Spirit gives me desire *for* God and his Word. (John 4:24)
- When I realize that I am learning to pray. The Holy Spirit is the one who is drawing me to communicate with God and to listen to him. (Romans 8:15)
- When I realize that I have discernment about a person or a subject – the sudden feeling of "Where did that come from?" as I express an opinion which suddenly seems very clear and obvious to me. (Ephesians 1:17)
- When my family, friends and church leaders recognize the Holy Spirit at work in my life. This will happen at different times and ways. A church leader might ask me to take up a particular role – my son might point out my unusual restraint in the way I describe his untidy room. (2 Corinthians 3:18)
- As I look back at regular times to see what God has been doing in my life – I do this at the New Year, my birthday and the anniversary of my conversion. (Galatians 5:16)
- As I encourage myself with the fact that everytime I recognize God working anywhere, I am experiencing the work of his Spirit in my life.
- Because I *know* that I am in the Kingdom of God. (Romans 8:16)

68 *Children and Evangelism*

4.5 How should adults recognize the work of God in children?

The most obvious indication of the work of God in the lives of children is that they are coming at all – to the group, to listen to you. There are usually a thousand and one other things they could be doing – but they are right there. They may be there for a hundred and one different reasons, but they are there hearing the gospel.

It is true, though, that for the leaders of the regular groups or members of the evangelism team, life becomes far more complicated when they start to recognize the work of the Holy Spirit and want to make sure that their evangelism or nurturing is allowing him to work. Some of them are too aware of the different "party" groups in their church to ask the questions. This is a shame because if the questions are not asked and therefore no answers suggested, everyone will settle for the lowest common denominator in their teaching about the Holy Spirit.

Questions which leaders might ask:
- Will children show the presence of the Holy Spirit in terms of spiritual gifts?
- Which gifts will they be given?
- How will the gifts be exercised in the whole church if the children are tucked away in children's groups?
- How does a leader cope with a child who has been given a gift of which the leader has no experience?
- Can God really heal people through a child?
- How will I know that a child is speaking in tongues and what should I do?
- Should I stop the use of gifts until I see the evidence of fruit in the child's life?
- Can't I just tell them Bible stories? After all, if God wants to do "things like that" (filling children with his Holy Spirit) then won't he just get on with it?

Children will be less aware of the politics of the group than we are. Therefore it seems that God often can work through his Holy Spirit in our children in a way which he cannot with us. I don't mean that this will necessarily be more flamboyant or noisier. It simply means that it *may* be different from the way he is working in us. Of course, some children will be very aware of how the Holy Spirit is seen to be working in the lives of the adults around them and so their expectations – and therefore God's working – are likely to be similar to that adult evidence. I can afford to be relaxed about that.

I just need to go on teaching what the Bible teaches in a way which really communicates with children, and pray. God will then do his work. Where I cannot see it, I will learn to trust him.

Our difficulty is often that we want to protect children from being disappointed in God through having unspiritual expectations of him. But God can deal with those childish wrong expectations. Of course I am responsible to give children right teaching so that their expectations of God are right but that will take time. It is taking time in me, too. God is able to deal with them and with me as we learn to ask and go on asking. In evangelism with children, any coming from outside the church do not know the pattern of expectation in the church. We work on a totally clean canvas as far as church pattern is concerned. That's a really healthy start. If each of us had no examples in our mind of bad practice, we would all be far more ready for God to do what he wants to do anyway.

Be encouraged, these children will be really ready for God to work – but they may come to you for explanation of what God is doing. Remember that the Holy Spirit comes to a believer at conversion – he comes at all our times of our repentance and of God's forgiveness. We need to make sure that every child who comes to God knows that with real assurance and looks for and welcomes the evidence of his coming.

4.6 How will that evidence be presented in Christian children?

How will they recognize this presence of God in their lives? They will only learn as we are open with them about the signs of his presence which we can see as we share our own lives with them. If they learn to recognize his presence in our lives, they will then be ready to see him in their own. If they know what the Bible teaches us sure signs of the presence of the Holy Spirit, they will look for him to be there.

Consider for a moment a group of children who are already in the church and who know they are in the Kingdom. As you look at their lives in the same way as you look at your own, you will recognize God working there. As you look at their lives and recognize God working there, you should point out what you see so that they learn to recognize his hand and look for the work of the Holy Spirit too. This means that when their friends come to God for forgiveness and invite the Holy Spirit to live in them, the children you have nurtured will be the ones who then encourage others.

When you look at the children you are nurturing in your group look for the same things you look for in your own life:

- Are they showing a desire to get to know Jesus?
  - *that's the work of the Holy Spirit*.
- Are they showing hunger for the Bible and for prayer?
  - *that's the work of the Holy Spirit*.
- Do they come out in a matter-of-fact way with discerning comments?
  - *that's the work of the Holy Spirit*.
- Do they regard encouragement from you about what you see God doing in their lives as really important?
  - *that's the work of the Holy Spirit*.
- Are they able with your encouragement to look back

and see the change which Jesus has made in their
lives over a period of time?
– *that's the work of the Holy Spirit.*
• Are they growing in their assurance of salvation?
– *that's the work of the Holy Spirit.*

There are two particular areas in which adults have trouble
with the evidence of God in the lives of children. They are
two evidences which often need the understanding and
explanation of adult leaders to survive:

• *Tongues*. Children do not seem to get "hung up" on the
gift of tongues in the way adults do. Children who have
come to me about this have often come in some bewilderment
asking, "Why is it that I say words that I don't know when
I am talking to Jesus?"

I ask them, "Is it a word here and there that you don't
know or a whole sentence of words?"

The answer usually is something like this, "It's lots of
words – I run out of what to say and how to say it and then
I start saying words I don't know."

The way to reassure them is to ask another question, like
"Well, does God enjoy the words you're using?"

This places the emphasis on God and away from the
assessment of a person. Their worship of God is acceptable
to God because he initiated it anyway. Then I find it easy to
explain that God sometimes gives us a new language. I
explain that the new language is a gift from him and he gives
it to us so that we can praise Jesus and so that we can pray
about things that we do not understand.

I encourage them to pray because God loves us to talk to
him. I encourage them to listen to God as they pray and to
leave time to listen to him *every time* they pray. The church
often forgets to teach that prayer is listening as well as talking, but to a child who has just come into the Kingdom, this
is wonderfully sensible and often ties in with praying in
tongues – after all, praising God when you don't have to
think what you are saying leaves you free to listen to him too.

I do not talk to children usually about the use of tongues in what is often called "prophecy" because that is not usually the situation they have come to see me about. I think that tongues in prophecy is a far more difficult topic to teach a child. There is the whole element of an "audience" to deal with. As soon as the Holy Spirit is working in a child's life in a way which would attract other children to copy, then we are into problems. It is of course a common problem with adults, too.

● *Pictures*. Often children who have been brought to faith without any knowledge of church jargon will introduce what I would call "a picture" by saying something like "It's a bit like . . ." and will then start describing a scene. This needs listening to. You might want to ask questions for further details because if they are excited they will leave out important things. Ask them questions in such a way that they do not feel under pressure to perform. You might say, "So who is standing behind you in the picture – or can't you see that from where you are?'

▷   Be prepared for the scene to be continued at a later stage. It might have a second part which will come to the child's mind the next day – do not presume that because it was not all given at once, the first part is the God-given part but the second part is their own imagination. It may all be valid.

▷   Do not try to draw too many teaching points from what they are telling you. Ask them what they think. Why does that help you with what we were reading today? So which of the characters in your mind do you think is most like Jesus? How are the other people behaving towards Jesus in your mind? Does seeing them help you in any way?

▷   Suggest that you pray together about what they have described. They may not have thought of the picture as being from God so it might be helpful to thank God for what they have thought about and to ask him to keep it safe. From my experience, visual images go on in the mind for a long time and can easily be replayed.

▷   Pray – when you are on your own – that you will be able to suggest Bible material which they might read with new understanding now. You might like to suggest a set of

short passages which they could read each day for the next
week which would help them to pursue the new thoughts
which are buzzing round their head as a result of this
picture.

4.7 How will God work through children's prayers?
Those who lead children's groups and BCEs usually fall into
one of two categories:
- those who discourage children praying for anything in
  which answers can be measured, and
- those who are looking for the miraculous all the time.

Sometimes children have asked me to pray with them for
something which I am not happy about. Perhaps this is
because I do not know the children and I am therefore reti-
cent about the follow-up this sort of prayer will have. I am
quite clear though that I *must* pray with them for what they
have asked. I do not consider that I have the authority to
pray for something different from the request of the child
simply by using different words in the prayer.

I am, however, free to ask them for more details about it
before I pray. Through these questions I should be able to
prepare the way to some extent for what I think they need
to know. It may be, for example, that they are asking God
for something which I know is not in keeping with his character to give. I *could* deliver a lecture on the character of God,
but this would go "in one ear and out the other" of any child
who had no experience of prayer or of God.

> If, instead of a lecture, I ask them questions about
> what might happen next–
> - what God might say when he hears their prayer,
> - what God is saying about the situation about which
>   they are praying even before they pray,
> - what God is saying about their own life as they come
>   to him to pray
> – the conversation will open up and their whole idea
> of what is happening changes.

They will then be far more open about what the Bible says about prayer and the way God sees it than if I had delivered my little lecture in the first place. The whole situation will have changed from a "Let's press this button and see what happens" approach – like a visit to the Science Museum – to a fascination with a subject which has captured many theologians.

It is important that children keep track of what they are asking in prayer and how they have seen different answers.
They need to be honest about the answers:
- the ones which they celebrate,
- the ones they do not understand,
- the ones which were exactly the opposite of what they wanted.

They need to be encouraged to go on thinking while they pray and not to assume that they will be still praying for exactly the same thing in six months' time. Train them to recognize that as they pray about a situation God is talking to them about it and helping them to see the situation from his perspective.

Unfortunately many children have caught the attitude to prayer that if you alter what you are praying because God has not said "Yes", this shows lack of faith. They will have heard that we need to "hang on in there" in prayer. Undoubtedly we are told to persevere in prayer – to ask and go on asking. But we need to listen and go on listening too. Unfortunately we are not so good at doing this because it requires much more effort.

From time to time it will be appropriate for:
- children to pray for children for forgiveness, help, freedom from fear, for healing.
  Encourage that, even though you may not hear the words you would have used yourself.

There will also be a growing number of occasions when:

- children will pray for leaders and
- leaders will pray for children.

When this is happening, try to be as matter-of-fact about it as possible.

There is no reason why everyone has to be involved in praying for one child – or leader – who is frightened about going to the dentist. When prayer is taking place, the group will be able to pray while others are clearing up or preparing something. A simple explanation will be given and the children will soon get used to this being a normal part of the life of the group and not something which is confined to "prayer-time".

4.8 What can we understand as we watch God's work with children?

We said earlier that often God works in a group in ways which are within the group's experience. So as these children, who may have been given the gift of tongues, join a group of people who also use that gift, they are likely to be given prophetic words for the group. It is important though that we deal with this as two gifts – one of tongues for private worship and one of tongues for public worship and prophecy. There are too many people around who have them muddled up. The principle is clear – teach what the Bible teaches and be matter-of-fact about the outworking of it.

So what about "pictures"?

I was brought up in a Brethren Assembly and everything I learnt about God from my parents was along strictly Brethren lines. So, I certainly knew nothing about "pictures". I now know, looking back, that I often had "pictures". These were waking dreams which showed me truth about God. How many of them were the product of a strong, visual imagination which God used, and how many were specifically *given* to me, I don't know – nor do I know if it is important. An imagination is not divided into two clearly defined areas – one which is spiritual and which God can use but the other secular. Many times, especially after I had accepted the

Christian faith as my own, I would be reading the Bible and come across something which I had seen in a "waking dream" at some earlier stage.

My waking dream

When I was perhaps eight or nine years old and had recently been taken to Horseguards' Parade in London, I had this "waking dream".

I was running across a parade ground in total panic and fear. I could see a group of vicious people with stones and I knew that they were out to get me. There was no escape. The only person with me was someone I presumed to be my father – he had taken me to Horseguards' Parade – and as the situation reached an unbelievable peak of fear, he pulled me round from beside him to stand behind him and underneath his overcoat.

I put my arms round his waist and hung on to the belt of his trousers so that I kept with him as he continued to run. Then I felt us turn as he faced the inevitable conflict. I could feel the sweat of his body and the heaving of his breath as he flinched. I could hear the crash of the stones the assailants were throwing and saw them roll past us on the ground beneath the overcoat. He groaned and swayed and at last crumpled and fell. I lay under the coat and I knew he was dead. I was crying and hot under the coat.

Everything was quiet so I crawled out and looked around. The parade ground was empty and unthreatening. The path towards which I had been heading, when disaster struck, now offered free access. The tears still ran down my face as I looked down at the dead body of the man.

Then I saw that the coat was empty and he was standing laughing down at me. Not my father – but another all-powerful, unable-to-be-beaten saviour. He swung me round him and we were both laughing as we ran towards the path.

I must have been about fifteen when the members of the Covenanters group to which I belonged started to learn Romans chapter 5 off by heart. Suddenly that "picture" I had had as a child leaped to life in my mind. I felt slightly embarrassed in the group as I reacted. The words from the authorized version stunned me as the waking dream ran again in my memory.

I felt again that fear and total helplessness and I felt the strength of the arm of the Lord as he swung me away from danger and under his cloak; my sin under his righteousness. I felt the agony of that death as he faced it with me hanging round him like a dead-weight. I saw again the huge granite lumps which had been meant for me rolling past my feet when he had taken their blow. I felt again the body slump in death as I rolled to the ground beside him in the overcoat. I lived again that moment of exhilarating joy as I was swung round by a living Lord not understanding my "free gift" but so exceedingly thankful for it. "For when we were yet without strength, in due time Christ died for the ungodly" in verse 6 and "saved from wrath through him" in verse 9 were both statements which I can remember as being so powerfully evocative.

It was only a "child's picture". But it not only taught me truth at a time when reading the written word was certainly duty, but also paved the way for the written word of God to have impact in what was another major turning point in my Christian life. Obviously I have picked out an example which in some ways is not truly representative as not all the pictures I had as a child were so stunning in their effect at the time and later. However I do know now that I had these waking dreams a lot as a child. The point is, without my visual imagination some spiritual truths would have had to wait for many more years before gaining any response from me.

4.9 What is the basis for assessing God's work in children?
The other difficulty we noted earlier is when people believe that God is present only when we are able to prove that he is – by strange phenomena. This is sad because we are ruling out a whole area of faith. God is at work among us because

he has *promised* to be. When we are reading his Word, when we are trying to understand it, when we are praising his name and when we are being together as the people of God – that is where God loves to be. We do not need to prove to each other, the children or those outside that he is there. We just need to enjoy his presence together.

We have looked at four important principles:
- Do not look continually for proof that God is working in a group.
- Live by faith and look confidently for him.
- Remove the "audience factor" as much as possible.
- Do not inhibit a child's faith by your own doubts.

When you ask God to work among the children in evangelism try to be honest and open about it. You are not listing ways in which you are prepared for him to work and others where you are not. Ask God each week to enlarge your faith and that of the other leaders working with you. Do not pick out some of the good things which you see God doing and promote them above others as you discuss them together as leaders.

The good things might be:
- A child has asked a question about something she has read in the Bible.
- A child has prayed for his granny and she died; he has expressed relief that she is out of pain and with God who can care for her.
- A child who has previously caused real discipline problems is starting to listen carefully during the Bible-time.
- A leader who has been praying privately for a child who is jumpy and nervous is approached by the parent for help with abuse.
- A child has asked you about a new language she is using when she prays.

Praise God for all these ways in which he is revealing himself among you. However if some of these are welcomed as being more exciting than others by the leaders, you will soon start to seek and promote those above others. Soon after this happens you will find that the children are beginning to recognize God among them in the ways which excite you – perhaps healings – but not in understanding his Word. This is catastrophic but it is happening in many of our churches.

We need to say clearly that the most important evidence of the work of the Holy Spirit of God in our lives is when we hunger after God and have a continuing appetite for his Word. If that goes, we are on dangerous ground and will quickly dive into heresy, taking our groups with us.

◊ **Looking back**
- What are you looking for in your life which will assure you that God is working there?
- What are you looking for in the lives of children which will assure you that God is working there?
- Are you living alongside children as God is working in their lives – making sure that you are working with him and not being an obstacle?
- How can you make sure that you are not defensive about gifts like tongues, healing, prayer?
- How can you make sure that you do not promote these gifts above others, both in your ministry and in your weighing up of what God is doing in the group?

◊ **Looking forward**
This brings this part of the book to an end. The second part is about planning evangelism. There are so many different ways in which evangelism can take place, ranging from one-to-one through to the big event. As a Budding Children's Evangelist look at all the different possibilities and imagine them happening where you are.

Part Two
PLANNING EVANGELISM

5

Settings for Evangelism

5.1 What are the general guidelines?

There are so many different ways in which to reach out to children with the Gospel, but only certain ways will be appropriate for the particular children in your area. It is important that we do not look at a model which has been successful in one church and think that if we lift it straight into our own situation, we are bound to be successful there too. That is not true. Nor is it true to think that if we get hold of the right person, or the right material, then that will guarantee our success. That is also wrong. We have already seen that our responsibility is to preach the Gospel making our method of presentation as appropriate as possible for our audience. The work of salvation belongs to God and the results are his responsibility.

We have already seen in 3.3 that the major influence on the life of a child is the family. One of the many factors which will influence your outreach will be the attitude of the parents in the area. If they are negative towards you or openly sneer at what is being done, your work will be an uphill struggle. If for whatever reason they are in favour of what you are providing for their children, your outreach can really make progress. When praying about your evangelism it is easy to be trapped into praying only for the children and their response. It would be more sensible to start by praying for their parents and their schools, since their attitudes are so often reflected in the children.

• *Ideas*
The possibilities for methods and vehicles to use in presenting the gospel to children are endless. Any idea you hear

about will need to be taken and adapted for your area and
your childen. All ideas should be seen as a springboard for
other ideas. Once you have the first, there is never any end
to ideas – they just spawn others. If you are in the initial
stages of thinking about these ideas, it is good to give yourself plenty of time.

Thinking and planning under pressure cause panic and
unwise decisions. Once you have made some decisions about
how you will start evangelism, don't stop thinking. People
who do so will be found still using the same methods and
approach in ten years' time. Continue to think and pray and
plan so that you have a continuing flow of ideas which will
motivate you and be appropriate for your children. We will
look at ten ideas in detail later in this chapter.

**So what are the main ideas which will start our imagin-
ations working?**
- Family evangelism
- Friendship evangelism
- Regular groups
- Regular church services
- Special services like Harvest, Christmas
- Children's home groups
- A mission
- Holiday Bible Club
- An inter-church event
- Christian holidays
- Events in schools

- *Planning*

We look at planning in more detail in Chapter 7. If you are
planning a new phase of evangelism with a group of people,
meet together well in advance. Your first meeting needs to
be long before the starting date and the first meeting of the
group can be a lot of fun. You can all start off by saying
"What could we do in our area, with the children we want
to reach, if there were no limit on time, money, people and

resources?" Then go for the ideas. Don't discard any of them.
Listen to all of them and note them down. There will be
plenty of time later for trimming them down to those particular ones which are right for your area now.

• *Communication*
The big rule is that as each decision is made it must be
communicated to the people it affects. The person who is
heading up the evangelism has the responsibility for making
sure this happens. We will be looking at more of those
responsibilities in 6.4 and 6.5. It is so easy to get the whole
area of communication wrong because:
– we presume that someone else has told the people concerned.
– we know that there will be other related decisions made
  and we leave people to hear them all at once.
– we feel that people may react badly so we put off the evil
  moment of telling them.
– we race on to the next scene of action and forget that such
  a momentous decision ever occupied our minds.
All very good reasons with one very bad result.
Poor communications lead to bad relationships.
And bad relationships lead to weak evangelism.

• *The Gospel – for evangelism and nurture*
One of the major difficulties most of us face as we plan, is
to present the Gospel clearly, while at the same time growing
the young Christians we have in the group. The answer is
to realize that there should not be a distinction between being
Bible teacher and being an evangelist. An evangelist should
be a responsible teacher of the Bible. After all, we often do
not know when evangelism is more appropriate than nurture. The trouble is that the evangelical divide of Christian/
non-Christian trips us up. Of course, we are either "in
Christ" or "without Christ" but there are some things which
do not change.
   If the Bible is being taught properly in the group then there
will be the challenge for right living, challenge for growth of
faith and challenge for forgiveness of sin for everyone –

leaders, children and those who have not come to a position of personal faith. This teaching will be presented in a wide variety of ways. We look at some of these in 7.2–7.7. In our regular groups, evangelism will often be defined by the response of the individual members rather than by a decision on our part to be an evangelist.

> ▷ **I am today in the same position I was in thirty-three years ago, when I came for the first time to a position of personal faith**:
>
> I need forgiveness – today.
> I need to be filled with the Holy Spirit of God – today.
> I need to learn from the Bible – today.
> I need to grow in my relationship with Jesus – today.

The synod report *Children in the Way* used the model of a pilgrimage for a picture of the Christian life. A pilgrim starts off each day in the same situation as the day before, making the effort to step out and choosing to go in the same direction. The pilgrim is one day's journey further down the road each morning but sets off in exactly the same way each day. This model is helpful when our planning and thinking becomes muddled over the Christian/non-Christian divide.

● *The team*
In this book, the people who are going to be involved in this evangelism is called your team. I have put aside the whole of Chapter 7 to look at the needs of the team and the way it works in different situations. That team may consist of you with one other person – or several. There are many gifts which ideally need to be represented on the team. There are different ways to collect your team together whatever kind of evangelism you are going to become involved in.

There are several options for the team structure:
- *Use only your own people.*

Look out. Be prepared to make mistakes, but it's worth it.

- *Use your own people but invite one or two specialists with experience in certain areas like music, drama, speaking.*

Look out. Communication about who is doing what is vital if the team is going to operate as one unit during the mission.

- *Use a full team from outside and do the promotion and follow-up yourselves.*

Look out. You might feel very much a spare part. You will need to be seen around a lot during the evangelism otherwise the follow-up will feel like a disjointed disappointment for all concerned.

- *Teaching materials*

So far in this chapter we have looked at:
- the ideas – different vehicles for evangelism.
- the planning group – the people who will make evangelism happen.
- communications – with all the other people who will be involved.
- the Gospel – the whole reason for what we are doing.
- the team – the people who are going to do the work.

Once these aspects have been settled, the teaching material must be chosen. The choice is:

- material produced by you for your own church – after all, you all know your church better than anyone else does.
- material produced by professionals – after all, they know more about mission materials than anyone else does.
- material which the professionals have produced but which you have adapted for your own church – this could be the best of both worlds.

Any evangelism takes time. Because of the way children learn and the things they love to do, there will always be many hours of preparation behind each hour spent with them.

A prime example of this is the person who is preparing the Bible material. They will need to be freed from other activities in order to prepare for this mammoth task. They will need the opportunity to discuss the Bible passages they are using with other members of the team, or with your clergy, so that the material is thoroughly truthful to the Bible and appropriate for the age-group concerned.

● *Finance*

One of the constraints which dictates the type of evangelism you plan will be the finance which is available for it. For example, you cannot hold an event which needs complicated lighting and sound equipment, specialist art/craft materials and professional drama props if you have only £150 to spend in your evangelism budget.

In fact, the financial manoeuvring with your leadership team or PCC should be headed up by one person who has done some preliminary costing and already has the respect of that group on financial matters. It should be said that in most church budgets the money for children's work is at the bottom of the list of priorities – many churches do not even have a specific budget for it. They simply expect the leaders to finance the resources they need themselves. In terms of evangelism this is not feasible.

Maybe the church really does not have the money to free a large sum for children and evangelism. In this case it will be necessary to hold a gift day or to ask for giving for evangelism over the whole period of time in which the planning for it takes place.

● *Aims*

Aims can be short-term and long-term. For example, your long-term aim may be to contact the children of every home in your area over the next five years. An individual event you organise may form part of this. You will then have short-term aims which are for that one event.

You will have to decide whether such an event is going to:
- be an example of church life together.
- be an opportunity to celebrate and explain a Christian festival;
- be an opportunity for explaining who Christians are and for inviting children to come into the Kingdom.

Of course there are many others too. They are all very different and you need to be clear about your aims before you start.

When you have decided on that aim, stick to it and make clear to the people in your congregation what the aim is. Then they will have realistic expectations of the event. Otherwise, they will either invite children to come who are ready to hear the gospel, only to find no gospel is explained, or they will invite children to come to a party and find to their embarrassment that they are given a detailed presentation and asked for a response. Either situation can be upsetting and is unnecessary.

5.2 What is the structure for organising evangelism?
Having looked at the general principles involved, we can now consider how to set up the structure so that good and appropriate evangelism can take place.

Before you start a new phase of evangelism:
- Invite a planning group to take control.
- Decide what needs to happen and when.
- Advertise the event in places frequented by the people you are inviting.
- Decide the age span you are catering for.
- Plan appropriate activities, food and decorations for that age span.
- Decide on your presentation of the Gospel at that event in terms of its evangelistic impact.

> It could be – initial social contact with church
>   – showing the Christian faith
>   – explaining the Christian faith
>   – giving opportunity to respond to the
>   gospel

The planning group
- The planning group will need to know whether they are planning a long-term strategy or one event which needs to meet a short-term aim within a larger plan. If they are planning such an event, explain how it fits into longer-term objectives.
- They will need to know the budget for the event. They will need to know whether it is to cover its own cost, whether only the church families are going to pay, and how the tickets are to be priced for say children, students, adults, senior citizens.
- They will also need to know where the event is to take place and any fixed points in the event, who will be presenting the Gospel and how long that presentation will take.
- They will then need to plan the entire occasion with timing and logistics of any general movements, like how to get everyone to a certain place for refreshments.
- The choice of age-group is important. Planning a general event without thinking about age-groups will mean that the event will cater for no one rather than for everyone. You will not know whether to play snooker or The Farmer's in his Den, to eat beefburgers and crisps, or beef stroganov. The whole thing will leave everyone trying to work out whether they were supposed to be there at all. So before the planning group meets, decide who they need to target.

This planning group should have a core of people who are prepared to think and pray about the event. Of course this sounds obvious, but it is surprising how many mistakes we make because we have not worked out basic principles before everyone else became involved. Once the team is galvanised into action it is too late – decisions are made and action taken and we all end up making the best of a bad job. We need a group of thinking people who know the age-group and the area where the work is being done. They may be able to delegate all the work, but their decisions and thought will stop that work being useless.

So once . . .
the thinking people have worked out the shape and type of event, they can then expand to be . . .
the planning group to sort out the arrangements and the team.

This planning group will need to refer back frequently to the people who have done the initial thinking. The planning group should be made up of a selection of people, not necessarily an already close-knit group. They will then have access to . . .
a wide variety of people with different gifts to bring to the event they are planning.

Usually when we are overwhelmed by a new project or initiative we start from the small, safe ideas. Then it is very hard to move out from there. Instead, we thought in 5.1 about how to start with the huge and often impossible ideas. Then gradually draw the boundary in until you have a shape which is the right size for your particular resources and situation. You are likely to find yourselves being far more adventurous.

Rather than starting from, say, a budget of £5
   – with a team of three
   – in one room
   – with 500 children
   you can go for all the really cool ideas.

Do we have to be adventurous? Yes, I think we do. I think it is impossible for God to direct us unless we say that we will do anything he wants us to do. That *is* being adventurous. By starting with the big and ludicrous ideas and slowly drawing the boundary in, we are actively showing God that we will do what he wants us to do. So let's be adventurous now as we look at the possibilities of evangelism with children. We'll look at each of the ten ways which were listed in 5.1.

5.3 How do families operate in evangelism?

As we put the child into context of society, we saw that the family was the biggest influence and provides the closest relationships for any child. We know of so much strain being placed on today's marriages and families. We certainly would want to be seen as a group of people who are promoting, and not weakening, those relationships. We also know that any child who comes into the Kingdom of God without the support and encouragement of the family will have a struggle.

In the context of evangelism there are two ways in which the family is an important unit.

- The family is the God-given place for the Christian faith to be explained and modelled to its own members.
- The family is the ideal unit to explain and model the Christian faith to other families.

So as we continually bear in mind the family which every child represents, we will take every opportunity to encourage the family to support the child's faith. We can also see that any opportunities to reach other *whole* families should be welcomed and taken with enthusiasm.

This is easier for some people than for others. If you have children and one of them is friends with a child of another family, it is the most natural thing for those two families to get to know each other. It's natural – but it's not effortless. The way to encourage the relationship between the two children is to exchange invitations to each other's homes. So long as the two homes are in the same area this will automatically happen. You will just find that your child is asking their friend to play and being asked to tea in their home too. But to change that into contact between the whole of your family and the whole of theirs will take a lot of prayer and planning.

You may find that hospitality is the most straightforward way – to invite the parents of your child's friend in for a coffee when they come to fetch their child. Or perhaps to invite the family to a family meal if the other children in their family are of a compatible age to your own. In most cases, be prepared for a long-term commitment before you can invite them to anything which is at the church. But even if you find the relationship with the parents slow to grow, at least they will have a background of knowledge of your family when their child is invited to go with your child to any church event. They will know someone to contact if there is anything which has worried them about what their child has been taught.

However long-term it seems, do not lose sight of the aim – that the whole family will come with your whole family to worship God together. Find some way of reminding each other about this, otherwise the prayer and effort will slowly dwindle. Your expectation and effort to explain the Gospel in small ways will stop. As we get to know people well who do not have a faith, we become used to them the way they are and we lose the imagination for their coming to faith in Christ. Keep hold of it in reaching out to families.

Of course, when you reach out to children you will not know all their families personally like this. Many of them will be totally unknown to anyone in the team. That is why in all the children's evangelism we plan, we must keep their parents in our minds continually. Many churches use the school holidays as a time when they launch into children's evangelism. It is important that in the contact you have with any parents, both in and outside the church, you make the aims of the event clear. You will find otherwise that the event is being treated as a Play Scheme and they may not accept that there will be Bible teaching and spiritual challenge as a high priority in the programme. So whatever your contact with parents, make sure that you tell them straight. Put it on the handbills, the posters, and mention it continually in prayer requests in the church. Make it very clear when you issue a personal invitation for children whose families you are getting to know, that your aims are spiritual ones for their children.

This honesty is not simply to save us embarrassment when their children go home and talk about what they have learnt. Parents have the first responsibility for their children and nowadays are, quite rightly, far more wary about entrusting their children to unknown adults – even in the church. Our honesty is also important because their child is their responsibility before God. God has given *them* their children and will therefore hold *them* responsible for their spiritual development. We need to be very careful that we do not try to take away from parents this responsibility – even though some parents will be quite relieved to give it to us.

One area of witness for the Christian family is the local schools. Our own families in the church need to be encouraged to be seen around their local schools in any appropriate way. Some of them may feel that if their own children have moved on to higher education they no longer have a link with the school, but this often makes it easier to be a visitor there. Your own children may take some while to get used to your being a regular adult around the place and some children always prefer to keep school and home separate. One of my sons, at five, obviously found my regular visits to his school reassuring while the other was quite disturbed by them – especially on the one occasion when I was supply-teacher for his class. Encourage any members of your church who are around during school hours to find an appropriate way in which to contribute to the life of the local school. See paragraph 5.12 for more detailed ideas.

5.4 What is friendship evangelism?
Friendship evangelism has many similarities to family evangelism. It is using relationships which arise naturally from where you live or work, in order to explain and live out your commitment to Jesus. In the case of children's evangelism, it means you will back up friendships which the church children have with other children.

For example, you may hear that a child from a church family is friends at school with the child of someone you work with:

- Start praying for the person you work with.
- Ask the Holy Spirit to stir your imagination for the change which Jesus would bring into your colleague's life.
- Ask for opportunities be more involved with that person, perhaps through sport or other activities outside work. Build the relationship, being encouraged that this is also being built from the other side by the friendship between the children.
- Make the opportunity *when appropriate* to drop in, phone or write to keep contact.
- Look for other links, perhaps through the Parent-Teacher Association or other services the church provides such as a Parent and Toddler group, or the uniformed organisations.

Relationships are the first area of successful evangelism. So many people, when explaining how they came into the Kingdom of God, will speak of a friend who just patiently lived and chatted the Gospel over a long period of time; ready for opportunities but enjoying a real friendship with a real person. These friendships between adults can help the Christian children who are experiencing their early efforts to spread the good news. They will know that they are supported within a framework of real friendships which are spreading the Good News.

5.5 How can we use our regular groups?

The regular children's groups which meet in our church every week can be a starting point for evangelism. After all, these groups give regular contact with children, often with the same team of adults each week. The most obvious way in which a Christian child can use friendship evangelism is to invite friends to come to an enjoyable group in the church.

Unfortunately, in many churches these groups still have the old Sunday School image and this can be unattractive for a newcomer. They are also likely to aim for the nurture of the children in the Kingdom rather than explaining the Gospel to those who are unfamiliar with it.

To be usable for evangelism, our children's groups must cater for the wide spectrum of experience which a Bible teacher should be catering for in any adult congregation:

- those who know,
- those who don't know,
- those who are spiritually hungry,
- those who have lived on spiritual convenience foods for too long.

They are all there in our groups amongst our church children. We cannot opt out by saying that we are dealing with nurture and cannot be expected to "do evangelism" too. The trouble is that the regular children's groups in many of our churches need a thorough overhaul but there are few people who want to be bothered to do that.

We need regular groups for our church children which:
- have leaders who are showing real spiritual growth,
- have leaders who prepare the Bible material as thoroughly as they would if they were going to teach it to the adults from their pulpit,
- have leaders who have regular training in the skills needed to do this,
- have leaders who are thoroughly familiar with this generation,
- meet in a room which is attractive and welcoming.
- are clearly recognised, by the church, as part of the church.

When this is the situation, there is no reason why the group should not prove to be the ideal starting point for children's evangelism. Evangelism is the normal responsibility of any church so there should be no need for us to alter completely every "normal" activity in order to do it. If the group is functioning properly, led by motivated adults, Christian children will be bringing their friends to enjoy it too.

5.6 How can we use our regular church services?
Sometimes it is hard to realise that our churches are supposed to exist for those who are not yet members of them. For the most part, the language, ritual and aims are tailor-made for the already initiated. Maybe you have sat in services in your church which had been advertised as being evangelistic and thought, "Thank goodness I didn't bring anyone."

Please do not give up. If the best way for a child to come into the Kingdom is in the company of the rest of the family, then it seems logical for there to be a place for them to come, *together*, into the church family. We need to keep reminding those who make decisions in our churches what the people out in the ordinary world are really like.

The activities of worship in your service will need to reflect in some way the type of person you are expecting to come. For example, if you live in an area where people would willingly turn up to listen to a PTA speaker about the school curriculum, then it is possible that they would listen to a 25-minute sermon. If, on the other hand, the most demanding public address the average member of your area listens to is the sports news – which is lively, fast-moving and illustrated – they are not likely to be impressed or interested by the sermon at all.

One colleague I took to church whispered to me as the collection plate came round in the closing hymn, "Is this for my rent?"

She felt she had been there that long by then.

Of course the church has responsibility for its members, too. We need spiritual food and we all need those times in our church which are just for the members of it – but we have become self-indulgent. The activities of our churches are often those which have been going on for the last fifty years and not those which are appropriate for the people who are walking by outside. Unless we continually comment on and discuss the decisions which are made about future activities, everything will stay as it has been done before. Then the families of the children we are reaching out to will be invited into a church which will feel outdated even to the grandparents. Certainly we need to be careful how we do this questioning and discussing of plans in the church. For example, how would newcomers find your family service?

Does the programme for a family service include explanations and help for those who may be there for the first time?

• *Music*

Are the hymns familiar and traditional – ones which newcomers might know from schooldays?

Are they new, modern songs which they might find attractive?

Are these introduced in a way which would help people to learn them?

Is the accompaniment competently played on an appropriate instrument?

• *Bible teaching*

Is the Bible reading from a translation which would make sense to any listener?

Is it read well so that it holds your attention pleasurably?

Are the notices kept short?

Are there other items which help those unused to sermon-type communications to concentrate and understand – like drama, use of OHP, illustrations from personal testimony?

Is the sermon interesting? Does it deal with a subject which would be universally appropriate? Is it presented in language which the speaker would use when talking about any other subject?

Thinking through something as familiar as your own church service with a newcomer in mind is not easy – because to you it is so familiar. It will take time and continuing effort to make the Gospel accessible to newcomers through your regular church service.

5.7 How can we use our special church services?
There are various festivals in the church year which lend themselves quite naturally to family celebrations and events. Traditionally these have been times like Harvest, Christmas, or the Church Anniversary. In the last few years because of concern over the overtly occult celebration of All Hallow E'en, alternative parties have been offered by churches on the evening before All Saints' Day. Each of these festivals – and many others like them – give the opportunity for us to celebrate with other members of the Kingdom of God.

They also offer tremendous opportunities to explain how and why the church celebrates to our neighbours and their children. In the Old Testament, the celebration of the festivals was never only for the people of God. It was for all those who were involved in the community life of God's people.

In Deuteronomy 16 the list of people invited to attend the celebrations for the Feast of Weeks (verses 9–12) and then the Feast of Tabernacles (verses 13–15) goes like this: you, your sons and daughters, your menservants and maidservants, the Levites in your towns, and the aliens, the fatherless and the widows living among you. The festival was for everyone who lived there and who wanted to be part of it.

The festivals of the people of Israel, which were a regular part of living as God's people in an alien world, were to include any people from that alien world who wanted to be there. It was the way in which God's people could show and explain what God had done, and encouraged them to celebrate the festivals with them.

Why don't we look on festivals like that too? If our times of celebration do not attract and instruct the rest of the world about the gospel, what will? As in Deuteronomy, these festivals are ideal times for family because children were an integral part of all that God gave his ancient people. So as we celebrate the festivals let's think "family and non-members", as they did. Let's use these opportunities to explain the gospel and live out its truth together.

Through the year with the church family might look like this:

● *New Year*

Use the theme of making resolutions as you start the new year. This gives you the opportunity to explain that the only way for a real new start is when God makes us a new creation.

● *Look at Lent*

Use the theme of taking time to think. Many churches invite people to special groups which take time to look at Christianity and to study the Bible. Make sure that there are appropriate groups for the children and for teenagers too.

● *Mothering Sunday*

Use the theme of servanthood. This is an opportunity to introduce the Suffering Servant who took on the role of serving the lowliest in order to reveal God to people. Invite children in the service to collect a small posy of flowers for their parents or the person who cares for them.

● *Palm Sunday*

Take to the streets. Lead a time of singing and praise in your local streets and take the opportunity to explain that Jesus came to die. The children can make large palm branches while a Pathfinder group in charge of a real donkey has to be seen to be believed.

● *Good Friday*

Look for every way in which the sombre mood of this day can be reflected in what is worn, what is eaten, what is said and done. Often the emphasis is on quiet reflection and this is not felt to be appropriate for children and families from outside the church. Widen the creative activities and give families from outside the church the opportunity to reflect too – in creative arts, in meals as well as in a quiet service.

- *Easter Day*

Look again at the widest possible way to show the joy and triumph of Easter. The joy of Easter can be expressed in as many different ways as the joy of Christmas – but this rarely happens in the church. The message of the empty tomb and big old hymns are at the centre of the festival but a party is even more appropriate at Easter than at Christmas – children should certainly have a present to remember from the church at Easter time. Introducing baby animals and beautiful flowers into the building can open up the conversation – an incubator of baby chicks has a startling effect at an Easter celebration.

- *Pentecost*

The festival of Pentecost is easy to celebrate – although hard to teach accurately. The hall or church can be decorated with huge flames; great fun can be had with a wind machine; songs of joy and welcome are satisfying to sing and the message of Pentecost is the final part of the message of Jesus Christ.

- *Harvest*

It is on this festival that we give thanks and remember those who are without. Many missionary societies produce materials which can be used with children and young people as well as ideas for making this a family occasion – which of course, traditionally, it is. The harvest barn dance is a good activity to cut across the age barriers and food still attracts everyone.

- *Advent*

To celebrate Christmas without celebrating Advent is like not knowing that your birthday is tomorrow – you would feel cheated. Anticipation is an important aspect of our lives. To anticipate Christmas is to enjoy it fully

when it arrives. Teach Advent properly and know that
people are responding to the glory of God and to the
promise of the Second Coming. This is especially important now that so few churches take the opportunity to
teach the Ascension.
● *Christmas*
Please celebrate Christmas at the festival and not in the
middle of January. How are small children to associate
the party and the fun with the message if we leave
three weeks between the two? Tell the message at the
party – the whole idea of a festival is that it is a *celebration
of truth*.

Of course, different festivals call for different sorts of celebration and this will affect the way in which you arrange
and publicise the event. It may be that you are concerned
about the high profile given to Hallowe'en at the local junior
school. In this case you will be concentrating on that particular age-group even though there will be small items in the
programme which will be for small brothers and sisters,
parents, grandparents. The way the event is planned and
publicised will make it clear to families that this event will
be a winner for junior school children, but the tickets are
only available as family tickets for four people. In this way
you are saying that you are expecting them to bring their
junior school age child in a group of four people of different
ages.

Another festival, like Harvest, may have a more traditionally understood image and the publicity may simply be an
invitation card put through doors in the area. This could
invite families to your harvest service and to see the church
beautifully decorated.

In whatever way people are invited to the festival, the aim
is the same: that in celebrating they will see and hear what
God has done and be given the opportunity to become part
of his Kingdom.

5.8 How can we use the home group model?

We have looked at church occasions which share the life of the church with whole families, but smaller groups are usually the ideal way in which to build relationships. There are few people who prefer to be part of a large group unless they have a particular reason for wanting to be anonymous. Children are not exceptions to this. So when we have a small group of children meeting in a home setting to which they have been personally invited, we are probably in the ideal setting for evangelism.

It is in this setting that relationships grow most naturally in all three directions. They grow between children and children, between children and adult and between children and God. God planned his world to be made up of supportive groups around each child called families. In home groups it is as though we become surrogate families for a short time to other people's children.

Parental contact is so much more straightforward in this situation too. The invitation is coming not from a faceless group but from another child's parent to their child – even though it must be made clear that in this case the parent is representing the local church. When there is any reaction from the parents, they know who to talk to because they will have already visited the home of the adult when delivering or fetching their child. It is easy and natural too to invite the adults to other church activities which would be appropriate for them, because the relationship is there. You can work on the supposition that they will want to find out about the Gospel their children are hearing.

The home groups can meet regularly, but not necessarily frequently, depending on the average social life of the children around you. The group may be a weekly feature in a deprived area but may only meet once a month in other places. The important thing is that it is a regular event and an organised system. Children whose parents are outside the church will find these groups easier than groups which meet on a Sunday. Their family life will be far more flexible about a group which meets after school in the week than one which operates in the middle of a day during the weekend.

One reason why home groups can be a helpful setting for sharing the Gospel is that the home is a very safe place to be for most people. So when children come to faith and receive forgiveness and the Holy Spirit they will feel safe. This is so important because what to us is very familiar ground, will be amazing and possibly intimidating for them. Some who come to faith may even draw back for a while as they realise the huge decision they have made and will need the support of the group to think this through.

Some children will dance into the Kingdom but others will want to know:
- What will happen when God lives in me?
- Will you still know who I am?
- Will I do and say things which will make people laugh at me?
- Will my friends like me more – or less?

A girl in her early teens came to fetch her small friend who was praying with me at the end of a week's mission. The child had prayed that God would forgive her and make her life clean and that God would fill her with his Holy Spirit. As she finished, I asked the teenager what she thought about all this. She said, "Oh I know all about it – I did that too but I'm not a Christian now."

I asked her why she said that and she answered with real anger, "Well, have you told her everything – have you told her how the Holy Spirit changes you?"

I said, "Yes, that's what we have just been talking about before we prayed. Sally wants to stop fighting with her brother and she thinks that now the Holy Spirit is in her, God will make them friends."

The teenager said aggressively, "That's right, that's what happened to me. I was really bad before I became a Christian and then the Holy Spirit came and changed me and I was so good at school that no one thought I was any fun any more so I told him to go away."

That teenager needed the support of a small group in a safe home so that she could talk about what had happened. She was confused and angry. Her expectations had been partly right – what she had asked God to do in the first place, he had done. But the new person she had become was no longer the popular person at the centre of everything in school, and she did not like that new person.

We were able to introduce her to a Pathfinder group where this confusion could be talked through, but how much better it would have been if she had been introduced to a small group in the first place. Out of your evangelism may come enough reaction and real response to the Gospel to warrant the forming of a group which is especially for those who are new in their faith. This will be a safe place where the difficulties, and joys, of Christian growth can be examined and understood.

A group for new Christians would probably look at:
- the gospel.
- the choice which the child has made,
- the promises which God has made,
- the practical living of the Christian life.

These groups for new Christians are also much easier to run if they are home-based. Parents will be much more open to the whole idea if one adult can see them, explain what will happen and when, even invite them to look through the material which is to be used. Many parents will welcome this opportunity and for the leader it has exciting potential – to bring the parents through to faith, too.

Ideally such a group should be led by someone who can be released from their normal commitments in the church for some time. Although the group will be a short-term programme lasting perhaps six to eight consecutive weeks, the leaders may well be on demand for much longer. They will be the obvious people for children to come back to afterwards for on-going help and advice, for encouragement and prayer.

They will also be the ones the parents will come to, either for personal help or perhaps for help with their child, who may suddenly be a different person. This can be a real problem as children start the Christian life and find it impossible to explain their feelings or what has happened, to their own parents. The leaders of the group may be able to give help in this situation, especially if they have regular contact with the parents through running the group in the home. More about this is said in Chapter 8.

So whether the home group operates for long-term contact or for a short-term nurture course, children benefit from being part of a small group in a home. We have already seen in Chapter 1 how important it is to take a child's questions seriously and answer them honestly. This is much easier to do in a home group setting than in a big group, or a group in a big hall. The home group means that we will have time and privacy to answer the questions. We may also be there as God comes into a life. Then we will be able to give assurance and encouragement if no change appears to have taken place. We will also be there if God shows his presence in the child with tears, laughing, a barrage of questions, a flow of praying which might include tongues, a sudden burst of physical energy. Our home is a good safe place for a child to make a response to God.

5.9 What is a mission?

A mission is a special series of events specifically aiming to explain the Gospel to people who have not previously expressed faith in Christ. The aim for the mission needs to be decided before any planning takes place.

> **One of the first decisions when planning a children's mission is about the age-group you want to reach.**
> - If you want to bring as many children as possible of any age into the church buildings from the neighbourhood, say so in your aim.
> - If you want to concentrate on the sevens-to-tens age-

group but you are quite happy for them to bring younger children along if they look after them, say so in your aim.

- If you want to concentrate on a small group for ten-year-olds based around a computer workshop, be that specific in your aim.

Remember that there is not an ideal aim – it's simply that if you aim at nothing you will probably achieve nothing.

Time

Missions are time-consuming events. They can come in all shapes and sizes but it would be difficult to imagine one taking place with all the team still working full-time in their daily employment. A mission takes more concentration and energy than that. Certainly there will be people needed during the planning and preparation stages who can be available during the daytime, for example, to visit schools, the printers, and to collect together any specialist equipment needed. During the actual event many of the team will need to be available during the day. Some people may be willing to take a week of their annual leave – although it certainly will not be a holiday – in order to be around to go into schools and to prepare for the main event each day.

The Team

Having said all that, it is obvious why some churches invite an organisation to come in to do the mission for them – Saltmine Trust, Scripture Union, Ishmael, to name a few possibilities. These people are in great demand and it is important, if you are going to depend on that sort of input, to book them early. You will need to contact them eighteen months to two years before the event.

5.10 Is a mission different from a Holiday Bible Club?

Many of the issues relevant to a mission apply to a Holiday Bible Club. These events became very popular in the mid-1960s and are still used widely now. Although the Holiday Bible Club was originally aimed at evangelism it has become more widely used as a way of nurturing children of the church and in this it is very successful. Because of its approach to teaching the Bible from a broad base of interests, it has had a good effect on many of the old Sunday Schools which have taken on a new image after a Bible Club has been held.

Unfortunately, its influence can go in the other direction, too. One of the problems of a Holiday Bible Club is that it can be seen by some as a "Sunday School" every day. This is not especially attractive to children from outside the church – or inside it, for that matter. Even if the Holiday Bible Club model is used, it is probably better not to advertise it as that. As an enticing title to an exciting event it leaves something to be desired. A title introducing the main theme but with information on the publicity about the use of Bible stories will prove more attractive – and easier for children to own.

One advantage of using the idea of a Holiday Bible Club is that, as it has been around a while, there is plenty of material to choose from. Scripture Union bring out a new Holiday Bible Club programme each year and there are others offered by people like the Salvation Army. The Bible teaching material from the Church Pastoral Aid Society (CPAS) includes material for a Holiday Bible Club at the back of each of the thirty-two books in the scheme.

On the face of it these two events sound the same. In practice they are quite different. A mission tends to be more for evangelism than nurture. A Holiday Bible Club tends to be more for nurture than for evangelism.

Obviously these are sweeping generalisations. There have been many missions where the main work has been in the church, and many Holiday Bible Clubs where lots of children have come into the Kingdom. Yet the difference remains and it will be in our minds as we plan and prepare. The aim with which we start will, and should, colour our thinking all the way through. If we are going to make evangelism our top priority in an event, we must say so in our aim and refer to that aim whenever we make a decision.

In that way we will make sure that we do not start off thinking about proclaiming the Gospel to those who have never heard and end up re-telling it to children who hear the Gospel regularly. Both are valid activities, but one of them needs to be decided upon from the beginning of your planning.

5.11 What are the possibilities of an inter-church event?
So far, the evangelism we have been talking about has been based in the local church. That is not an accident – it is, in fact, where evangelism should be centred. But one of the big advantages to the one-off event we are now going to consider is that it provides an excellent opportunity for churches to work together by holding an evangelistic event.

You could book a central place which is well known to everyone in the area and arrange for various churches to take responsibility for different parts of the event: the music, drama, tickets, publicity and so on. The main difficulty with such an event is for the different churches to agree on the aim of the event and who should be invited to speak. It helps if the committee dealing with these points is made up of like-minded people, otherwise its meetings never develop beyond the initial stages of planning.

A few years ago, two such events were run in Birmingham under the auspices of Scripture Union. They involved several churches in the presentation of the gospel through the story of the impossible building of Jerusalem in "Nehemiah and the five-mile wall" and then the story of the flood in "One Way Ticket to Ararat". Children and young people filled as many roles as possible and worked in groups through the months of preparation. The gospel was explained by a Scripture Union evangelist.

For each of these events, the full team met only twice. The first meeting was early on in the preparations so that each small group dealing with music, or drama, or costumes, could see how its part linked into the rest. This took most of a day and was held in a church hall. The second occasion was one full dress-rehearsal on the morning of the event. "Nehemiah" took place in the Central Hall in Birmingham

and "Ararat" in the Town Hall. Both events were sold out
and it was difficult to know who benefited the most – the
audience, which was made up of families and children's
group, or the participants.

We all experienced home-grown evangelism in a way
which changed our lives. No one church could have held
such an event, drawing as it did on such a huge number of
people and skills, yet every church was important. All the
churches could own the event by inviting families and
children's groups to come to it. Young people prepared the
drama; others worked as clowns; children in a choir led the
singing. All of us experienced the panic, fun and demand of
evangelism. We prayed and planned together and encouraged each other to look to God for response.

5.12 How can Christian holidays be used?

Many people look back to a Christian holiday when they
came to faith in Christ. Many from a Christian background
recall that it was the opportunity to go away from home and
to understand for the first time that the faith of their parents
was one which they wanted to own themselves. The time
away with a group of people who you see not just for the
Christian content of the holiday, but for all the other activities
too, is the ideal way for the Christian faith to be both
explained and modelled.

As leaders of holidays we need to be aware of a heavy
responsibility – not simply because they are away from home
but because they are away from their church. With smaller
children we are very aware of being in *loco parentis*. But
with any age-group we are also standing for their church.
Evangelism and the nurture of faith were given to the family
within the context of the bigger family of God's people. As
a holiday team we are a short-term offshoot of that bigger
family. We must be careful to teach and live and explain the
Bible in such a way that the child or teenager goes back to
the local church feeling more at home – not more detached.
It can be one of the most difficult responsibilities to carry.

We know so little about the children and young people
who come on our holidays. Even on a parish holiday, where

more and more churches are seeing the need to provide an outside team to lead the children and young people, the team will see little of the child in context of the family. The home church may have been asked to give some sort of introduction to the holiday leaders, but there is really no way of short-cutting the process of getting to know the members of the holiday as quickly as possible. It means effort, commitment and prayer – and a willingness to be known by them ourselves. It is only as this process of mutual openness gets under way that the gospel will be heard and understood.

You can take your group away within a centrally run holiday with CPAS Ventures or with Scripture Union holidays. Or you could take your group away on their own. There are places which cater for groups and keep their cost – and therefore their facilities – down to a minimum. Most CPAS and SU holidays use boarding school premises and these often have swimming pools and other sports facilities. Christian Camping International maintains a computer index of residential venues. They will also give help and practical advice and training.

This brings us back to the function of questions and answers in exploring the faith. One of the many ways in which a Christian holiday promotes spiritual growth is by providing the opportunity to ask and consider questions. There is time on holiday to consider spiritual issues deeply and not simply to speak out the obvious answer. This is why the Christian holiday is the place where leaders grow and mature – as well as the place where new spiritual life begins and grows in children and young people.

5.13 What about schools?

Many people have looked to schools as the ideal place in which to introduce the Gospel. Schools are the obvious place in which to find all the local children. Some visitors may even see going into schools as an easy option because other professional people there take responsibility for discipline and practical difficulties. Unfortunately, these visitors not only do not understand the situation in a school but are in danger of spoiling any contact between school and church.

Children are required to be in school by law. The law also requires certain education to be administered and places the responsibility for this education into the hands of professional teaching staff. This produces a framework and structure for learning and for living in community life, which any parent who has children living under our nation's laws must be able to trust. These parents will represent all the different nationalities in the UK and therefore all the variety of religious life too. No one therefore is allowed by law to go into a school in order to propagate their own religion. As a Christian, I should be very glad about this, because that should mean that no one has been allowed to go into the schools where my children have been pupils to propagate a particular religious dogma.

> **It is wrong** to think of schools as a suitable forum for mission.
> **It is right** to want strong links between the school and the church.
> **It is wrong** to talk to everyone in a school as though they were Christians.
> **It is right** to take any opportunities we are offered to explain why we are Christians.

Assemblies

Some people are approached by the school to lead assemblies. Often these are the clergy and ministers of local churches known to the schools. Sometimes schools will also welcome other people who are not titled as ministers or clergy but who show that they have something of interest to say to that age-group. Occasionally, clergy who have had links with a school over a number of years will introduce another person to the school to represent their church.

If you are interested in pursuing this, please do not dive in at the deep end. Links with schools are grown over a period of years and are built on relationships. When we go into school we are contributing to the life of the school which will then go on for the rest of the time without us. So it would be arrogant to think that we can just walk in and do our own thing regardless of the reaction of the Head or other staff.

Taking assemblies is a skill in its own right. Of course, you need the ability to communicate in front of a large group. You need to be able to speak clearly and to use vocabulary which is suitable for that age-group. You also need to be able to speak for a very few minutes and still say something thought-provoking – something which will cause discussion and reaction, not confusion and dilemma.

People who take assemblies must make clear the perspective from which they are speaking. I say regularly, "Because I am a Christian . . ." This means that the children are not put in a situation of dilemma by what I say – they can dismiss it if it is against what their parents say. If, however, what I am saying is true about faith or spirituality in general, then I try to make that clear too. I might say, "All of us, whatever our faith is called . . ." I might list the different faiths represented in the school and include "those who do not follow a faith which has a name". When I pray at the end of assembly I explain that "I am going to pray in the name of Jesus. You may not be able to do that – but you can still listen."

The themes for assemblies are as varied as life. There are many new books about assembly themes which have suddenly appeared on the market with the coming of the new curriculum. The choice can be confusing. Have a good browse round the bookshop first to see the variety available. Then watch an experienced person take an assembly in the school where you have been invited. Now go back to the shop to choose a book which will be the most helpful in that situation.

Aim, in what you plan and do, to raise the profile of your church in the school generally. This will be a tremendous encouragement to any Christian staff and children there. It will also mean that when the church runs events to which it would be appropriate to invite the school, the links are there. Everything you do in that school needs to be done sensitively and with wisdom – if not, others may well spend years repairing the damage.

Parental involvement
We have already seen in 5.3 that one of the ideal links between the church and the school is through Christian parents. This lays down a foundation for any outreach which will take place between church and families, or children and children. When the church and the church families are seen to be reliable and open, then the gospel is more likely to be heard and considered. The main encouragement we can give to parents who have links with local schools is to pursue these at any level. The church needs to be seen around school life far more than it is. The possibilities for involvement are endless – and our presence in the schools will be welcomed.

As pressure builds on today's teachers to fulfil administrative as well as educational roles, so more outside help is needed for the more mundane duties of running a school. In primary schools this may be in the form of library duties, helping with sport or craft. Parents may find a way in by being the extra adult on the weekly swimming pool run or as the occasional visitor to accompany a school visit.

Governors
For the same reason, the opening for Christians to become school Governors should be taken up. In the last few years the role of the school Governor has changed. It includes more responsibility and power and therefore training. You may have people in your congregation who should be released by the church to function as school Governors. The role of Governor is both demanding and time-consuming. It would be difficult for someone to be a school Governor and also to play a major role in the church. People who have opportunity to fill this office need to know the support and understanding of their church and clergy before taking it on – they will often not be around at church events because of their duties as a Governor and therefore cannot ask regularly for the prayer they need.

5.14 What about prayer?

Whatever your method of evangelism and whatever your aims, you will need continual prayer. This needs to be promoted and supported by those planning the evangelism. The prayer needs to be directed through the normal church channels and must be regular and informed. There is always a dilemma between the rest of the church feeling they are being left in ignorance about the arrangements, or feeling saturated with information. In our church, we never seem to get this balance right. A mixture of information spoken up-front in a service, and written, attractive sheets of paper which can be taken away seems to work best. It is easy to be so busy with the doing that we do not pray. When we stop praying we then stop encouraging others to pray.

Evangelism is something to DO

Evangelism is one of those subjects about which it is really easy to run courses, listen to speakers, watch examples, talk of needs and even write books. None of these things will make any difference to the children who need to know about Jesus in your area. The only thing you can do which will make that difference is – get involved. Evangelism is something to DO.

◊ **Looking back**

I have given only ten examples of what must be hundreds of different possibilities for evangelism. I do not know your area, the type of children you have, the sort of resources which are available, but you do. Or rather you should.

So look back now at the selection and choose something for your area. But please, *please*, don't do *nothing*.

◊ **Looking forward**

The next chapter is about where to start. Perhaps you think all this sounds fine for the large, affluent, influential churches. You have been trying to imagine evangelism happening in your struggling community and found that hard. You cannot do it on your own. That's why the next chapter explains the way to find a team. The team may be only one other person or it may be a whole group. Delve into the next chapter for some encouragement.

6

Choosing, Training
and Leading the Team

6.1 The good news and the bad news

Leading a team of leaders involved in evangelism is one of the most frustrating, satisfying, enjoyable and daunting jobs around. I experienced the daunting aspect the first time I led a children's mission at my own church. I sat in the Team Time during that first afternoon, before the children were due to arrive, with my stomach in knots.

I had suddenly realized that although there were several of us on the team who had been involved in this *sort* of thing before, we had never been involved in the *same* mission before. How did I know when I described an activity to the team that we were all imagining the same thing? So how could I be sure – without doing it all myself – that it would all happen the way I wanted it to? The answer, of course, was that I couldn't – and that was why my stomach was in a knot.

Of course, I knew that I didn't *want* to do it all myself. I genuinely wanted us to be a team; for us all to be involved in a way which reflected our gifts and our level of confidence. But for the next thirty minutes before the children arrived, until I really knew in experience that we could all operate as a team, life was going to be painful.

We have run several events since then and there has never been that awful feeling again. Even though new people become involved, and different people run it, there are always some of us who have worked together before and who know what we are each talking about. I don't think I shall ever forget that afternoon and I do now know that the responsibility of leading a team of leaders is not all joy.

But it is fun. The relationship which grows between people

who work together in evangelism is unique. To go through the traumas and the battle; to see signs of God working in children and in each other; to live in a constant attitude of prayer and spiritual preparation and to survive days where without God and his sense of humour all would be lost – this produces relationships which are like gold.

> **The stages of preparing a team for children's evangelism are:**
> - collect your team together
> - learn how to lead them
> - decide on appropriate training for them

We shall look not only at the way in which to choose, collect and train your team. We shall also turn our attention of the job of being leaders worthy of this splendid group of committed people. We will look at the way in which we can make sure that the high standards with which we began will continue as we work together.

6.2 What does the Bible say about team members?

Whether your team is one other person or a group of twenty, how do you start to collect your team members together? The Bible shows us what we should be looking for.

> Reading the whole of 1 Timothy will help to focus on what the Bible says about team members. At least read 1 Timothy 4:6–16 carefully. It talks about leaders in the church. And all the people who end up on your team will be leaders of one kind or another.

Paul gave Timothy in chapter 4 verse 6, a dual-purpose outlook in the evangelism team he was heading up:
- He was to go on following the good teaching and truth in which he had been brought up.

- He was to point out this way to the people in the church in Ephesus who were working with him.

The situation in Ephesus was just like ours. There were people who were without Christ and who needed to hear the Gospel; there were others who were Christians who were working together as a team to tell them the gospel. So this Bible pattern suggests two things we should aim to do:
- to go on growing and learning ourselves.
- to hand on what we already know to others.

Look at what Paul is telling Timothy to value in himself and in "the brothers", that is, the team:
- godliness (verse 7)
- spiritual fitness (verse 8)
- devotion to godly activity (verse 12)
- recognition of own gifts (verse 14)
- patience in practising gifts (verse 14)
- time to practise gifts (verse 14)
- attitude of a follower (Ephesians 5:21–6:9)
- single-focus mind (verse 7)

The Bible shows us God's rules and guidelines for living and serving in the Christian life. Here we see his rules and guidelines for living and serving as members of a team for evangelism. We need to take careful note and to set our own standards on the same lines.

Some try to opt out of what the Bible is saying by arguing that:
- We don't mean the same things now when we talk about the spread of the Gospel as Paul did when he wrote to Timothy.
- It's different because we are living in the West.
- It's different because we are not first-century Christians.

– Paul's standards are so high that only the keenest
follower could reach them.
**But this is God's way we are talking about, and
therefore it is the only way for people who take evangelism seriously.**

So we shall look at each of these attributes of team members which Timothy was to look for and train. As we look at
each one we will be setting our sights on God's high standards for our team, too – whether that is two people or
twenty. In the letter to Timothy he is given no space to settle
for mediocrity – but there is room for all the gifts which God
had given to the whole church. We need to know what these
qualities are so that we can look for them in ourselves and
our fellow believers and so that we can encourage each other
to progress and grow as we see how high the standards are.
We'll work our way down that list.

• *Godliness and spiritual fitness*
These two qualities are not always assumed to be necessary.
It may sound surprising, but it is often true that people offer
to be involved in an evangelism team when they are not
living godly lives themselves. This is especially true for evangelism with children, since children's work is often seen as
safe areas for those who are unsure of their faith.

Of course these two, godliness and spiritual fitness, mean
the same thing. Unfortunately, not everyone in the church
is spiritually fit. There are those who do not read and study
their Bibles any more because they think they know its contents so well or cannot be bothered. There are those who
have forgotten about praying in faith. There are those who
no longer have a hunger for spiritual things – or for
righteousness.

• *Devotion to godly activity*
You may feel appalled at having to decide whether others
are devoted to godly activity or not. After all, we are only too

well aware of our own spiritual weakness and deficiencies, so how can we start to gauge others?

> Here in 1 Timothy, Paul talks about the sort of people who show evidence of a spiritual life. They are people whose lives are an example to others "in speech, in life, in love, in faith and in purity".

As the leader of the team, you need to show discernment about the lives of others – while being humble and honest about your own. We have said that the two ways Timothy was to lead was to go on growing himself and to hand on to others what he already knew. In the same way, you will need to show discernment about your own spiritual state, listening to the opinions of your elders in the church, and then discernment about members of your team.

Looking for people who are involved in godly activity does not mean that you look for the person who is on every church committee, runs the visiting team and works in the local Christian bookshop. Quite the opposite, in fact, because that person is unlikely to have the time and commitment you are going to require. It would be wiser to look for someone who shows real enjoyment in personal study of the Bible and also in being with children. It may be someone who regularly and quietly encourages others in the church. Ask that person to think and pray about joining the team.

● *Time and patience*
You are looking for people who will be prepared to give time. You may not need them all to be on committees or working parties, and you may not be holding an extended event or working as a team over a long period of time. But what you are expecting of yourself is what you are asking of them – a commitment in preparation and in prayer, which will take time.

It is important to make this clear from the very beginning. People may need to take annual leave or set aside a certain amount of time every week in a busy schedule in order to be well prepared for the event. This may sound obvious but we are again in the area where people may think, "Oh it won't take long – I've only got the under-fives."

The word Paul uses as he talks to Timothy about his preparation for using his gift is best translated "devotion".

In 1 Timothy 4:13 Timothy is told which activities will need devotion. He is also told the result of such devotion will be that other people recognize the progress he is making.

Unfortunately it is often the people who are making no progress who offer to be involved in an evangelistic activity. Perhaps they become aware of spiritual dryness and feel that rubbing shoulders with some enthusiastic leaders will change their own condition. This is true – praise God, that is what usually happens. The danger is that the opposite *could* happen and those who started with spiritual fitness and buoyancy could end up feeling drained and empty. So be careful how many people you encourage to become involved whom you feel uneasy about. Be prayerful about the choice and also about the role you ask them to play.

● *Prepared to follow*
It was not only Timothy who received these instructions. The church he was working with in the city of Ephesus also received a letter from Paul so that they knew God expected them to follow and to be good team-members.

Look at Ephesians 5:21–6:9.
Paul tells the church members in Ephesus that in order for the Kingdom of God to be extended in Ephesus, they need to work together and not against each other. They need to know who has responsibility and care for others. They need to learn to follow and to obey.

Timothy, like any other leader, needed people who were prepared to follow his example. Many of us find following difficult. The emphasis on knowing our rights in society has stressed our position as individuals, so that being one of a group following someone else can be difficult. Paul makes it clear in the letter he sent to Timothy's team that following was vitally important.

● *Single-minded*
This means being single-minded about following Jesus – not single-minded about evangelism. We can be eager to take off in any new direction and give it our full attention while it has novelty value. Others may see us as committed and spiritual but God knows when our eyes and direction have gone from his Son – to something about his Son. That is not the same thing.

> **Evangelism and children** are subjects which can move people deeply.
> They need to.
> But they are never to replace the need to keep our eyes on Jesus. They are not the latest novelty interest to replace or bolster our relationship with him.

6.3 What are the characteristics of a suitable team member?
When the leader of a team is looking for prospective members, there may be confusion when they see gifted and willing people who do not come into the spiritual categories we have outlined in 1 Timothy.

They may be really good with children and have a lot of time available. Church leaders may consider that an adult who is not in the Kingdom will benefit from experiencing children's evangelism and so they encourage them to be involved. The leader of the team may feel very wary, wondering how to include such people without weakening the impact of the evangelism.

It is true that when people are spectators at a Christian

event for children they are often far more open to what they are hearing than when they know that a preacher is speaking to them. This is one of the exciting realities of a service for all age groups. The danger, however, is that in wanting them to be there to hear the gospel we might forget the main aim of the event – to bring children to a knowledge of salvation. This aim is not likely to be achieved if the majority of team members do not have a real knowledge of that salvation themselves.

It *is* possible to have unbelieving adults involved in supporting roles in an evangelistic event, but it is vital that their areas of responsibility are made clear – to them and to the rest of the team. They must never be in a situation, for example, where children might go to them for spiritual help, or to verbalise a response to the Gospel. They can often be involved in publicity, craft work and practical preparations. There must never be a situation where other team members are inhibited because they feel that the only adults around them are unbelieving people.

So:
- Strictly limit the number of such people you will have.
- Make clear to the team throughout the event what their roles are.
- Have someone on the team whose job is to care for these members.

They may want to make a response to God themselves. You cannot have leaders tied up in conversation with other adults, when they are actually there to spend time with children.

This all sounds very clinical and exclusive. I am suggesting we need to have a loving, sensitive but clear-cut attitude in this situation. The gospel *is* exclusive. A person is either in Christ or not. If they are not, they cannot give help to someone who wants to belong to his Kingdom.

The team leader will look for three indications of a healthy team:
- **Strength.** You'll find this in the *sameness* of the members of the team. They are all on the team because they are disciples of Jesus. They are working with a common aim

and they have a common need – to be equipped to do the job God has given them. They will need encouragement to support and affirm each other.

- **Wealth.** You'll find this in the *variety* of characters on the team. Each is bringing to the team an individual personality as well as individual skills. They will need encouragement to be themselves, knowing that it is why you wanted them on the team in the first place. If they stop being themselves, they impoverish the team.
- **Growth.** You'll see this in the *lives* which are lived out alongside your own. Ask God to renew your eyesight so that you see him working. You will see this happen within an event and also from year to year in different events. People will change and surprise you – and so will the team as people come and go. There will often be unsettling change but then the evidence of growth and progress.

Some people you approach about involvement in evangelism will be very unsure about their gifts. They may have become stuck in the rut of serving in one particular way in the church. They may feel comfortable with children but never thought of it as a gift. If as you pray for the event you find your attention being drawn towards people like this, do go and talk to them. They may need to see things from another person's perspective. Tell them what you are looking for in the team and the particular characteristics that have attracted you to them. Then leave them to think and to pray about the decision.

Do not put pressure on them by:
- making them feel that you, personally, need support
- telling them that you are sure God has sent you to them
- making it impossible for them to say "No"
- asking for an immediate reply

Before you approach any new team members, decide what you will do when people offer to be on the team who are totally unsuitable. This is an extremely difficult situation and someone in authority in the church may need to come into the discussion. Ask people to pray about giving team members the right job to do and for help in dealing with any who feel that the job you offer does not reflect their gifts and abilities.

You don't want people on the team who should not be there, or who are not sure that they should be there. The difference in their support and motivation compared with people who have made a spiritual decision to join the team is considerable. It is noticeable in the way they work in the team, the way in which they relate to the children but most of all in the preparation which they are prepared to do.

- You may have people on your team who know nothing about children. That's not ideal but you will survive if they are intent on knowing Jesus.
- You may have people on your team who have never been involved in evangelism before. Perhaps they have only recently come to faith themselves. If they are single-minded about being disciples of Jesus, the team will be strong because of them.
- Of course we need expertise about children and about evangelism, but we must get our priorities right and realize that we are disciples first – then children's evangelists.

You need people on the team who understand that the time and effort needed in preparation are not to please you, nor to run a successful event, nor to prove that they are capable of doing a more prominent job than the one you gave them.

They give that time so that the evidence of the life of the Holy Spirit is seen more clearly in their lives.

6.4 What are your needs as you lead the team?
Your needs as you lead the team are fundamentally important because if those are met you can then lead the rest of the team. So if there is someone you long to have working

with you and yet who is already doing much of the work in the church anyway, it *is* still worth making an approach. Explain what the event is and why you particularly want them on the team, explain that you know how busy they are and ask whether they could off-load one or two of their usual jobs for the period of the children's event.

This may result in your having someone working alongside you who is really experienced and supportive. Such a person may show real flair for this new job, or may go back to the previous job refreshed (if still needed) because of the change of thought and aim.

Above all else:
Pray for someone who will work alongside you as a real companion.

This needs ideally to be someone you can talk, laugh and pray with without any reserve.

Then thank God for this person every day, because this one will be your sanity – both in crisis *and* success.

The most important thing to remember as team leader is that you are leading a team of the followers of Jesus. They are only following *you* because they are following *him*. They are not a collection of clones you are cultivating. It is disastrous when leaders gather around themselves such a collection of like-minded people that the team becomes a "Yes-gang" for the leader.

Someone pointed out that Jesus does not break down differences between people, but bridges them. Jesus does not break down differences by making us all the same, but builds bridges so that our variety as a team becomes a strength and not a weakness. It takes a strong and mature leader to face that and work within it with equanimity. I find this a real struggle. I would much rather work with a team who think and work just like me because I then trust them and find them easy to predict. My mind tells me that this is stupid and that it makes for a bland, boring team with all my faults multiplied – but my emotions find that less threatening.

Paul is very clear in **1 Timothy** that certain gifts had been entrusted to Timothy.

He did not want Timothy to forget those gifts nor the way he had received them. The gifts had come from God.

Timothy had other gifts which he had not received by the laying on of hands. These gifts were presumably innate in his character. Otherwise why would Paul have chosen this young man as a leader?

There must have been other gifts which Timothy did not have at all.

The use of any gifts requires patience and perseverance. Some people who recognize that they enjoy certain areas of service and that God is using them in those areas in the church expect to be perfect within that sphere of work immediately. They seem to think that God only gives us gifts to play around with. Paul is obviously talking throughout the letter to Timothy about gifts which would grow into maturity.

If we recognize this, we shall not only look for a growing expertise in these areas but will also be willing to be placed in roles which reflect our present level of ability and experience. We shall be prepared to work at a humble level knowing that our gift will grow. The church seems to have too many prima donnas at the moment – people who recognize the gifts which God has given them and presume that these exempt them from involvement in any other areas or from working at the maturing of the gift.

Sometimes my awareness of the need to continue to make progress is highlighted by meeting someone whose gifts are more mature than mine. It sharpens my appetite for growth. Sometimes I meet someone who thinks and acts about children the way I used to – as a straightforward teacher. Then I realize that God has done some work already.

We may need the help of other people not only to recognize gifts but to have the patience to look for them to grow and mature. As friends encourage us and see change in the way we exercise a gift, we have renewed appetite for growth. The growth of the gift God has given us will then be given its right priority in our lives and we shall be prepared to set aside time for it.

Think back to Paul's attitude to Timothy's leadership.

The way Paul saw the situation was this: only as Timothy walked the right way would the people follow him in the right path.

Often mistakes are made in leadership because the leader is directing operations rather than leading the way. This may work well in secular situations but not in evangelism.

It is wrong to complain of team members who
– are not praying,
– are unwilling to be trained,
– treat the whole event as an ego trip,
– have lost the imagination for what God might do,
– behave "off duty" in ways which are ungodly, if that is the way you are leading them yourself.

From the moment you take over the team leadership you can ask people to take responsibility for all sorts of practical arrangements, work and decisions. But you can never hand over the spiritual leadership. From the moment you step into the shoes of being leader, you are required to pray, live a godly life, exercise faith in prayer and decisions and look for growth in yourself and in the members of the team. The only parallel to this is the preparation of the athlete for an event. We have all heard of people who are "too heavenly minded to be of any earthly use". But the danger in leadership, especially in an event whose success can be measured by other people, is that we become too earthly minded to be of any heavenly use.

6.5 How will following teach you to lead your team?

God's aim with Timothy was not simply to have a church which had good leadership but that his work would be seen in Timothy's life at the same time. Every effort which Timothy made was for God and his church. To do that, as we have seen, he had to concentrate on his own godliness as a top priority otherwise he would lead others astray.

Paul says to Timothy at the end of 1 Timothy 6:
"But you, man of God, flee from all this, and pursue righteousness, godliness, faith, love, endurance and gentleness.
Fight the good fight of faith.
Take hold of the eternal life to which you were called in the presence of many witnesses."

It is only as the gifts of godliness grow in us that we can lead others in them. It is only as we learn to follow that we become ready to lead others. So the commitment we make to our own walk with God returns full dividends even though it often is not a smooth learning curve. Sometimes I come away from a training session I have run and know that it's gone much more smoothly than I had any right to expect – I had not prepared it thoroughly. Other times I feel well prepared and yet nothing seems to go right and I come away feeling useless. So where is the sense in the pattern and where are the full dividends which we get back for the time put in? They are found in the way in which our lives show the life of the Holy Spirit more and more. That is God's work and we can trust him to do it.

People are sometimes seen manipulating themselves into leadership in the church because they find following so difficult to do themselves. We may let them become leaders because they seem less hassle that way – for the time being. Unfortunately, this only delays the hassle. Someone who cannot follow or recognize authority becomes the worst kind of leader. An important indication that the Holy Spirit is working in our lives is that we become good followers. He will then grow that gift of following by making us into a leader.

One good thing I inherited from my Brethren roots is my attitude to discipline and leadership. I know that I am a rebel by nature. It only needs someone to lay down the law about what I must do, or must not do, for something inside me to retort, "Who says so?" The word "mandatory" to me is a word which provokes revolt and I have to make a conscious decision to obey speed restrictions which carry that word.

Although this personality trait caused friction between my parents and me, there was certainly no way in which I was allowed to get away with it. There was no question about who was the boss in our home and – as the youngest by several years of four children – it certainly wasn't me. I was brought up in our assembly, and later in the village, under the strict understanding that the only people who were equipped to lead were those who had learnt to follow with grace and obedience. I still know that that is true even though I always find it difficult.

6.6 How do I grow as a leader for my team?

Although growth from following to leading sounds a gentle process, growing as a leader can be a traumatic experience because much of the learning experience is done in public. We have all been taught that we learn from our mistakes but that does not make us feel better at the time of making them. The team you lead will see when you make mistakes. Many of them will feel encouraged by your mistakes because they will realize you are on a learning curve, just as they are. Some of them may be fairly rough with you about your mistakes simply because by their nature they kick people when they are down – or maybe they happened to take the brunt of your mistake.

Many of the mistakes of leadership are because:
- decisions have been made too quickly,
- responsibility for work has not been handed over to others,

- the obvious, rather than the pertinent, decision was made,
- the leader reacted to the situation, rather than to the people,
- the leader forgot he or she was a spiritual, not secular, leader.

My most vivid memory of a painful mistake happened because I had "a finger in too many pies". The church was running an evangelistic outreach programme in one week which involved concurrent events for three age-groups. I knew what was happening in all the events – because I was a leader of the combined event – and muddled them up in my mind. As a result, someone spent time writing drama scripts which were not needed at all. I even helped him write them. What a fool I felt and how justifiably cross he was. I learnt from that mistake to wear blinkers when there is a lot of action going on and to concentrate on my own area of responsibility – even though I know I am missing out on some of the other fun.

Here are ten suggestions to limit your mistakes:
- Choose the team spiritually in the first place.
- Push secular attitudes to planning out of the way.
- Never make practical arrangements for the team which cut across their normal access to spiritual nurture.
- Keep your main aim for the event continually in your mind.
- Set yourself the personal challenge to focus on prayer in a way you never have before.
- Keep your own standards of godliness high throughout the time.
- Be realistic about yourself, others – and God.
- Provoke your own hunger for training.

> • Help individuals on the team to assess their own training needs.
> • Assess the training needs of the team as a whole.
> **We'll look at this list in more detail below.**

One of the things which we each need to do is to recognize the gifts God has given us. Why is it so much easier to recognize someone else's gift, rather than our own? Perhaps because it is terribly British to play down what we are good at and then feel offended because others have not noticed our gift without it being pointed out to them.

Recognizing the gifts which God has given us is not being big-headed about ourselves. It is quite the opposite. When I look at a skill which is needed in leadership and say, "Yes, that is something I can do," I am actually giving glory to God who made me, redeemed me and renewed my life. It is also a moment of recognition that there are other skills which I do not have.

> **Let's look at some points in that list in a little more detail:**
> • *Put aside the secular attitude to planning.*
> There may well be times when, even in the face of important deadlines, you find yourself saying, "Let's just pause here and reconsider where we're going." The team may be baying for the next step but you know that somewhere something has veered away from the right direction. It takes courage to stop the momentum even when you are not quite sure what is wrong. We have looked at the godly way to lead and the biblical way to choose a team. It may be that these come under threat and you will need to take a stand and set the agenda against a secular attitude.
> • *Never make practical arrangements for the team which cut across their normal access to spiritual nurture.*

Obviously each of you on the team will need to consider
how your commitment to this event will cause you to
adjust the rest of your church life. But this must be left
as an individual decision. Do not convene meetings at
a time when your team usually go to their Home Groups
or the church prayer and praise service. If they depend
on something for their nurture normally, you are putting them in a dilemma by clashing with it.

● *Keep your main aim for the event in your mind.*

Write it out and put it next to the mirror you use every
day or stick it on the door of the food cupboard. If it
slides from *your* mind you can guarantee that no one
else will remember it. Quote it clearly on any prayer
cards which go to the rest of the church so that people
know how to pray not only in details but overall.

● *Set yourself the personal challenge to focus on prayer in a
way you never have before.*

How will you fit in that extra discipline to pray? Decide
from the beginning whether it will be by getting up
half an hour earlier or by having prayer reminders
pinned up in front of you while you exercise or wash
up.

Be warned though. At one mission I decided to pray
that extra time while I was jogging each day. One morning I was aware that an elderly gentleman, who was
exercising his dog along the promenade of this quiet
seaside town, had leapt to one side for me. I realized
that I had said some of my prayer out loud – probably
very "out loud" since I was out of breath in the sea
wind. The next morning I not only checked that my
prayers were silent but also changed my route in case
he was a man of routine. Unfortunately he had changed
his route too – we simply averted our faces.

● *Be realistic about yourself, others – and God.*

You are not suddenly going to become a perfect person
overnight and nor are the members of the team. We all
make mistakes and the bottom line of your team

relationships has to be love so that you can all make them safely.

Be realistic about God – he *is* perfect and powerful and always keeps his promises.

● *Look at the training needs you all have well ahead of time.* Otherwise you will find yourself saying "Next time, we must . . ." Right at the beginning set dates when training will take place. If possible, duplicate your training arrangements so that all the team can be expected to attend.

Talk to the more experienced members of the team before and during the event to find out whether they would appreciate more concentrated training through an outside agent.

Encourage these experienced people to talk to the newcomers in the team regularly throughout the event in order to encourage and to pass on their skills. Training on the job is vital for people who are just starting to learn evangelism.

6.7 What training is available?

Training is a word which terrifies many people unnecessarily. Training is simply the opportunity to gain the ability to perform a role. It can be through reading books, listening to someone who already performs it well, or working alongside someone. Ideally, it will include a mixture of these and be carried out over a period of time so that there is opportunity to try out what has been learnt – and then to learn some more.

Many of us are not clear about the reason we are being – or not being – trained. Some will feel that they have been professionally trained to work in a particular area so no further training can be necessary. Others feel that the word "training" is too heavy – they just want to learn a bit more about the subject. A few have a level of skill which other people envy but so much of it is instinctive that they are unable to explain the skill and pass it on to others.

Training in any skill comes into three categories:
- Training in order to explore a new area of interest.
- Training in order to extend and enhance a skill where there is already some experience and expertise.
- Training in an area of natural ability in order to gain the vocabulary and principles needed to pass it on to others.

6.8 How do you receive training?

Some training comes into our lives incidentally. Looking back over a period of time we will see growth in our lives from a mixture of experience, formal training and what we see as just life.

I can see stages of growth in my work with children:
- We lived in a town briefly between two bouts of village life. When I taught my first Sunday School class in a Brethren Assembly there at thirteen – wearing the required hat – I did so because there were children in that class from our housing estate. I wanted to help them. I do not remember enjoying it very much and I certainly had no help in preparation apart from within my family. In our home, you taught the Bible because you knew the Bible and other people did not. If you did not teach them, they went to hell and you would be held to account.
- When we returned to the village, I took over the 3s–5s group on Sunday mornings and I also helped my brother run a children's club during the week. It was the first time I noticed the difference Jesus makes when he comes into the life of a child – and so realized that salvation was not just in the future, when they were adults or in heaven, but it started now.
- Then when I went to college to train as a teacher I

not only realized how much I already knew about children – either from instinct or from these church experiences – but I also started to take up opportunities for learning more. I became involved in beach missions and my experience broadened as I learnt to work on a team with very different people who varied in their experience but all had the same aim.

- With the birth of my own children I had other issues to face. Pontificating about other people's offspring is quite different from living with your own. I suddenly found myself asking all the really important questions about the spiritual state of the unborn baby, the "right age" for conversion, what happened to babies who died before a full-term pregnancy, because these were issues which we were facing in our lives as parents. We certainly had no questions left about original sin as we lived with two small sons.

- About eight years ago I realized that God had done something in my life which did not happen to everyone or to every believer. I noticed that where I had always been interested in children, I now felt motivated towards them in a way which made everything else pale into insignificance. I could not believe the way in which they and their affairs were almost completely ignored even in lively family churches. I became really excited about putting the Gospel into words which a child can understand without losing any of its truth.

- And there are still many stages to go, I hope.

None of those occasions was important enough for other people to comment on them. Most of this change I am only aware of now, looking back. Occasionally, I have been aware of change taking place and that has been because I have had people around me, friends or family, to point it out. Much of this "training" gave me no further written qualifications but each situation has contributed to my qualification for the roles I now fill. At the time, I was just living the next stage of life.

As we lead a team we need to set the pattern of training. We must make it clear not only that we expect training to go on in all these ways in others and actively encourage it. We also need to make it clear that we need, welcome and receive training ourselves. There are always training situations into which we can put ourselves. Some leaders are too arrogant to make this happen – feeling that they know everything or that others will only have different (and therefore wrong) ideas from themselves.

In that case, they should not be surprised if they not only start to stagnate as a leader, but notice a reticence in their team towards training too. Such team leaders will be saying the things they have always said, doing the things they have always done and being the people they have always been. Growth in skills and in vision will have stopped and this will have a knock-on effect on the team too.

6.9 How can you train yourself?
Many of us need help to assess what our needs are. We may need encouragement to branch out from an area of activity where we feel confident, to receive training in another which is needed in the team. Our reaction may be, "Why not send someone else – why can't I do what I'm good at?" The fact is that when we have expertise in one area, it may open the door to a related skill. On the other hand, someone who has not recognized a gift, may feel blocked off from receiving training in a formal way through lack of confidence.

Basically there are three ways to receive training:
- On the job.
- In a series of short, perhaps unrelated, but regular training events.
- In a full-time course.

These are not mutually exclusive but they do tend to lead on from each other. It would be unusual for people to recognize suddenly that they want to teach children and so enrol on a full-time course. It is more likely that:

- They would become involved in helping in an event where other more experienced leaders would pass on skills informally.
- This might lead them to be enthusiastic enough to notice courses offered in their area by some of the training societies in the evening or on a Saturday morning.
- They would acquire a wealth of patchy training over perhaps two or three years before thinking about enrolling for a week's concentrated study on the subject.

Unfortunately, few people pursue their training aims quite so relentlessly as this. Many never move from the first one and after a while may even resent others handing on skills to them. They start to look on training as an insult to their skills gained by experience and therefore do not insult others by handing on even those skills to them. So, the flow of growth in the team grinds to a halt, until they leave after years on the team. This is a very difficult situation for the leader of the team.

6.10 D-I-Y – TeamTalk

If you detect a reticence towards training in your team, why not try one of the D-I-Y courses which are available? It is probably better to go for one with a wide base rather than one which deals only with evangelism among children. A course which includes general skills like "Working as a member of a team" or "How to communicate exactly what you mean" will give your members skills which will lead directly into evangelism too.

One such course, called "TeamTalk", is produced by the Youth and Children's Division at CPAS. It takes the form of nine magazines which slot together to form a training course for youth and children's leaders. The training it gives is active and biblical. Training sessions do not rely on a gifted and informed leader of the group – it really is D-I-Y. Because it is available in nine instalments, the style of training and material can be tried out with the first instalment before the rest of the course is obtained.

6.11 Who can help to train your team?

Many people offer training with children, some specifically in evangelism. Their arrangements for doing so will change from year to year. It is worth finding out the general pattern on offer, and also approaching them with your own needs to see how they can be met.

- Some offer evangelism training alongside the training they give in working generally with children in the church. Some offer evangelism training separately.
- Others offer residential courses of a week or more.
- Some give training on the basis of hands-on experience and will take people for a year to work alongside an expert in a church situation.
- Some will bring training to you and will produce a programme to reflect the needs of your team and your situation, while others will expect you to go to them.
- Others will provide a package which can be used in D-I-Y training.

Organisations which offer training courses include:
Church Pastoral Aid Society
Scripture Union
British Youth For Christ
Counties Evangelistic Work
Youth With A Mission
Agape
Crusaders
Oasis
London City Mission

There is certainly no shortage of opportunity for training. None of it is effortless and most of it will take some money and certainly time. Without it we can probably stagger on for some time but our own lives will stagnate and our ministry will lack its full impact. The trouble is that the more training you receive the more you realize how much there is to learn and therefore the more you want to have – so expect your team's appetite for training to grow with each taste of it. This will only be satisfied with long-term planning and financial backing.

◊ **Looking back**
You may think you are the only one there is to do all this. But don't panic.
- Look in 1 Kings 19:18. God said to Elijah when he felt like that: "I reserve seven thousand in Israel – all whose knees have not bowed down to Baal and all whose mouths have not kissed him." There were, in fact, plenty of God's people to do God's work.
- Spend time now praying that you will meet up with others who share your concern for evangelism. Pray that you will be clear what your first action should be.

◊ **Looking forward**
In the next chapter we look closely at the different ways of teaching the Bible to children so that they listen and can understand the gospel. There are lots of enjoyable, clear ways of doing this. None of them will be effortless but all of them will end up by producing growth in the team, the team leader and the children. So don't stop and feel there is only you and you cannot do it anyway. Believe that God has others in mind and believe that it will be fun.

ALL TOGETHER NOW!
by David Bell

What do Scramblers and CYFA leaders have in common? Do Pathfinder and Climber leaders have anything to learn from each other? Does anyone else care about the Explorer leaders?

Here is a selection of ideas to use when leaders of different age-groups get together. If you meet regularly you may like to pick one or two for each meeting. Or if you don't maybe they will inspire you to meet for the first time as a complete children's and youth team.

ALONG THE LINE

Tie a piece of string or clothes line across the room or between two chairs.

Divide the leaders into their age-groups and ask each group to think of some items connected in some way with their children/young people to hang from the line with clothes pegs.

You can use objects, pictures drawn or cut from magazines, words written on cards, or anything else that seems relevant. Have plenty of paper, pens, scissors, old church magazines, odds and ends, sellotape, etc., available for the groups to use.

Peg the items along the line in age-order, with the youngest group at one end and the oldest at the other. Allow time for everyone to look right along the line. Encourage leaders to ask questions about each other's contributions.

Sit everyone where they can see the whole line. Ask for comments on anything it shows about how children grow up in the church. Is there anything important that it does not show?

HEAD TO HEAD

Divide into pairs of leaders from different age-groups. Try to make sure that one or two pairs have a leader from the youngest and the oldest age-groups together (eg a Scrambler and a CYFA leader).

Call out questions one at a time for the pairs to discuss. After each question leave time for discussion, but say "Stop!" before the pairs have finished talking about it. Once you have read out the next question they have to start discussing that one until you call "Stop!" again.

Suggested questions:

What is the biggest similarity between your two groups?

◆

Pick one of the children in the younger age-group. What will they be like when they are in the older group?

◆

How many of the older group were in the younger group at your church when they were that age?

◆

Argue about which of your age-groups is easier to work with

◆

What is the funniest thing you can remember happening in each of your groups?

◆

Tell each other what you think is the most important contribution made by the other group to the church

◆

How does each of you usually feel just before your group meeting starts and just after it finishes?

◆

End with a time when everyone can pray quietly for the other person in the pair.

7

Doing Evangelism

7.1 No guarantee of success

For most of the time when I was growing up, my home was in a small Hertfordshire village where my parents had the responsibility for a little inter-denominational Mission Hall. There were five of us in the family at the time. Together with a young couple who rented the cottage next door while doing a course at London Bible College, we did all the work in the Mission Hall while holding down various jobs and, in my case, getting through school.

Towards the end of the time we were there, an evangelist, who was a friend of our family, came to the village, set up a marquee and ran a mission for both children and adults. As I walked down the lane to our home one day towards the end of that week, the evangelist came out to tell me that one of the wealthy, influential men in the village had come to the caravan the night before and come to faith in Christ.

I ran home and told my father. My father was a very self-contained, quietly humorous man. He had worked in that lonely situation for about ten years. He listened to what I said and then sat down on a chair in our huge, draughty, damp dining room and cried his heart out. I can remember standing in the doorway with the sun streaming into the room from behind me, still out of breath from running down the lane, the sounds of harvesting coming in through the open door, the old clock giving its irregular tick on the mantelpiece – and my dad, who never showed any emotion, crying. I learnt then something which I have never forgotten – that evangelism can be very painful.

The man who was converted became, over the next few months, a total religious fanatic. He left his wife and family, became a vagrant and eventually died in the fire of a derelict building. He was the only adult from that village, so far as we knew, who came to faith in Christ during our time there.

***

Facts to accept about evangelism:
- Evangelism is tough and can be totally and bewilderingly unrewarding.
- We proclaim the Gospel because it is true.
- We proclaim it in a way which is appropriate for the type and age of person who is listening to us because we really want them to understand.
- There is never any guarantee of success.

***

Knowing that there is such a hard road for the message to travel should motivate us to present it well. If we really want people to understand the gospel and we know that they are biased towards not hearing and not understanding, we will be prepared to make an extraordinary effort in order to do our job as evangelists as well as possible. We know that the message is not presented in a vacuum. It is in the setting of a place, a people and other activities. We'll start by looking at these other supporting activities and then at the message we have to tell.

7.2 What ingredients support the proclamation of the Gospel?

The message of the Gospel is the same for all people everywhere but the way we present it, and the supporting activities with which we surround it, will be different from area to area. A programme of evangelism devised for an inner-city church will be made with the children there in mind. The people who plan any evangelism programme should know the area and the children. They should be familiar with the schools, the type of work and activity the children are used to. A programme which is appropriate for the inner-city would not work in a plush, middle-class area. Activities for children in a disturbed area need changing regularly to keep their interest whereas children from more settled homes would be unhappy at being moved so often. They would want to settle down to an activity and produce somethng to show other people.

These ingredients can be safely regarded as appropriate for any programme and most children:
- Music
- Worship
- Bible teaching
- Workshops
- Opportunity to respond

It's the balance of these ingredients which will vary from place to place.

These five basic ingredients seem to form a framework in which the gospel can be explained. We'll look at each in turn to see the possibilities they present. It is important from the beginning to realize that we are not giving each of the five equal importance. While each one has a significant part to play, all must focus on the teaching we want to give. Our aim is that children understand the gospel. It is no good putting all our effort into one of the other ingredients and then wondering why the children are inattentive and restless during the Bible teaching.

- *Music*
When we see how the commercial world uses music, we cannot help but recognize its power. You may not be aware that you are listening to music as you buy your breakfast cereal, wait for your train or plane, wander around your car showroom or sit in the dentist's waiting room. You may not be aware of it, but those who play it know its power. Music has a dramatic effect on our attitudes, our reaction to diffi- culty and stress, and our handling of relationships. That effect varies with the type and the volume of music and on who we are.

Children are no different from adults in this reaction to music. Like us, they may be totally unaware of the fact that music is playing but their attitude to what is going on will be affected by the music. So playing boppy, energetic music as they arrive may give the impression that this will be great fun. On the other hand, playing quieter music may be reassuring to those who have had to pluck up courage to come through the door.

Music can be used with children in many different ways.
- *Music for them to make:*
  - They can use percussion instruments, tapes of music, instruments which they learn to play at school, to contribute to the music of the club or group.
- *Music for them to listen to:*
  - as they imagine a scene you are describing.
  - as they enjoy a song which they will learn later.
  - while you show them a clip of a video instead of using its sound track.
- *Music to set the theme on which the event hangs:*
  - This may be a theme song or a theme tune from a television series which evokes the right atmosphere.
  - It may have nothing spiritual in it at all. There is a tendency to feel that in a mission, everything must have spiritual content, which often means that the songs we use are banal and empty. It is difficult to write simple words expressing great truth without the words sounding trite. If we stuck to using a theme song and chose good songs about God we would do a lot better.
- *Music to encourage praise and lead children to worship God*:
  - The songs need to be chosen carefully and known by the adults and some of the children before they are used, otherwise the whole event ends up like "hymn practice at school".

- Check that the words are true and appropriate. If they are objective they will be true for all children. If they are subjective they will be true only for some. We should be wary of helping children to mouth words which will be appropriate only when they have come to God through Jesus.
- Some songs should be energetic and boppy so that the children can dance around to them.
- Some songs should be quiet and emphasise the holiness of God because children find those characteristics of God hard to put into words – just as we do.
- All songs need to be chosen bearing in mind that there is far more to the faith of all of us than we can find words for. Songs can help us express important facts and feelings.

Using music in an appropriate way can be helpful at all sorts of different times in the programme. The person who is leading the music should be a spiritual musician who understands children. This is not an easy combination of qualities to find but is very important. Children will find it difficult if the music they are experiencing leads them from quiet expressions of thanks to energetic expressions of praise followed by a theme song about travel. The music should lead the children through the programme to the point where they hear the Bible teaching – and then on from there in response to the Bible teaching. What we are talking about is worship.

7.3 When is worship, worship?
- When life is honouring to God. All creation bears the mark of the Creator and in that way brings honour to God. That is worship.
- Some of the people of creation have responded to God's grace with a conscious decision to bring honour to him. As we live our lives we worship him.
- In some moments of our lives we are particularly aware

of the desire to give honour to God. So we consciously direct our praise to God and we call that worship too.

We need to be aware of these aspects of worship as we are involved with children and evangelism.

- Children are God's creation and the beauty of that creation brings honour to him.
- As they spend time with us they can catch that desire to bring honour to God by specifically worshipping him with us.
- As they spend time with us they learn that God is looking for that decision of their will so that their lives are given over to honouring God. He wants them to invite his Spirit to touch their lives so that their lives are worship too.

Ways of expressing our worship.
In the times we use specifically to give praise to God:
We encourage each other to be aware that God is with us.
We remind each other of what he has done and has promised to do.
We direct our praise to him.
We expect to receive from him.
All this can be done using not only the form of music but also:

- *Silence* – Give children plenty of warning of this because it is not something which our modern society finds easy. Tell them about the next item on the programme, perhaps a song or a poem, and then say, "When that has finished you will find that everyone is very quiet. That is so that we each can tell God how we feel about what we have heard." Do not be too eager to break the silence – recognize that you will find it difficult too.
- *Dance* – Find out what experience of dance the children are likely to have had in school. Then you will know how confident they are likely to be in using it in worship. Making simple movements to words

from the Bible is the least threatening way of starting
– it is also a way which blends together the differing
skills and attitudes of children and adults.

- *Poetry* – Children will have varying experience of this
  too but even where they have very little, poetry is
  easy to introduce. In a mission, start off at the beginning of the week with a funny, short poem to introduce a theme. This might be so short that they will
  know it off by heart when you have said it through
  two or three times. Then use poetry on other days
  in different parts of the programme. Children love
  the sound of words which is why playground chants
  have always formed part of playground culture. By
  the end of the week you will be able to use thought-
  provoking poetry – they may even surprise you by
  writing some.

- *Reading* – People need to be reminded that reading
  aloud is a skill in itself. Look around your team for
  people with clear diction – the sort of people whose
  comments at meetings can he heard easily. Particularly notice voices which are not too shrill or slow.
  This could be combined with another activity. For
  example, you could suggest a short reading to bring
  a time of silence to an end.

- *Reciting* – The reading may be short enough to learn
  by heart so that paper and print do not clutter up
  the communication. If you recite a reading, make it
  very clear that these are the words written in the
  Bible and encourage them to read the passage for
  themselves afterwards. Use dramatic and choral
  readings to help children to listen and remember.

- *Pictures* – A child's world today seems to be completely made up of pictures encouraged by television,
  the use of the video as well as magazines available for
  every age-group. A large video screen can be well used
  in a mission for a variety of purposes, including the use
  of a large beautiful picture as a background to praise.

Dance movements can be used in order to learn a passage of scripture. The movements of our body make a unique impression on our ability to learn and remember. We used dance/mime movements to help us learn Psalm 46 with the children at one Mission. We used the Good News version of the Bible and the verses featured in a different way in our programme each day; sometimes they were part of a time of praise using songs and spoken prayer and sometimes they were part of the Bible event.

These are the movements we put to Psalm 46:4–7:

There is a river

that brings joy

clap

to the city of God

to the sacred house of the Most High.

God is in that city

and it will never be destroyed

at early dawn he will come to its aid.

Nations are terrified,

kingdoms are shaken: God thunders

and the earth dissolves.   The Lord Almighty is with us,

the God of Jacob is our refuge.

All these supporting activities can be used by children or
by leaders in order to:
- encourage each other
- direct praise
- raise our expectations.

It's a pity that they are not used more widely in all our
services. If they were, people – and certainly the children –
who come into the Kingdom through our evangelism would
not have quite such a massive culture shock on encountering
the rest of normal church. The normal praise and worship
would be accessible for them.

The reason for using them is that our presentation of the
gospel should be as clear as possible. There is no point in
using an activity which takes the full attention of every child,
if it leaves the team unable to present the Gospel clearly and

effectively. The other activities support and enhance the Bible teaching and we shall look at that now.

7.4 How do we teach the Bible in evangelism?

Unfortunately the teaching of the Bible to groups of children within our churches has become stuck with a model of teaching which was used in secular education up to the 1960s. It is a model of teaching which supposes that a person, and particularly a child, can learn only if they are made abundantly aware that someone wants to teach them something. The obvious way to make this clear is to insist that they sit down and listen to the teacher.

Although it is patently obvious that this is not true, and that there are many other more satisfactory ways in which humans learn, the theory persists. In most of the groups which meet in churches with the aim of adults handing on Christian information to children, the groups are static and are addressed from the front. We need to be very clear in our own minds that this is a basic educational misunderstanding before we enter into any evangelism with children.

We learn because we live.
If we live in a restricted or abused setting we will learn little of any long-term use to us.

If we live in a stimulating setting we will learn things of long-term value.

This is true in the Christian life too.

If we live among Christians, life can be stimulating and we will learn.

Or it can be insipid and we can remain undeveloped, learning little of long-term use.

Of course, there is always the danger of throwing the baby out with the bath-water. Many people assume that because the old style of teaching was from the front, we would not do that now. Of course we do. We need to teach in every possible way, and it would be silly to ignore its possibilities.

We all need to go on learning about the Bible and from the Bible. We all have a lot to hand on to others too. We can learn from children and they can learn from us. The big difference is that adults have a God-given responsibility to teach children; children teach adults without having the responsibility to do so.

How should we teach responsibly?
We need to pray continually:
- that as we run games and exhibit craft ideas, play a musical instrument and dress up as Nehemiah for a sketch, our lives will be teaching the truth of the gospel.
- that as we put that teaching into words we shall find appropriate and fascinating ways of explaining the gospel to the children.

You can in fact use almost anything. You may decide to teach the Bible from the front if you have a large group and interject this with the drama, or a reading or some children who have learnt some of the Bible off by heart. You may use illustrations or a video or interview a child. The important point is that everything is focused on your aim and everything you use is true to what the Bible says. You must make this focus happen – it will not happen automatically.

What we have said is:
▷ There is the danger of assuming that the teaching will be true to what the Bible says because the person who is teaching is a Christian. This is not true automatically.
▷ There is the danger of thinking that it does not matter so long as you have a Bible story, the programme is entertaining and the children enjoy it. This is not true automatically – we must be sure that we are explaining the gospel.
  Either of these attitudes will mean that you are opting out of the responsibility God has given you to teach the Bible to children.

> **Go through your talk with someone else** – it needs to
> be someone who:
> * understands the Bible,
> * understands children,
> * knows you well enough to be honest with you.

It is a pity that over the years a distinction has been made
between being "a Bible teacher" and being "an evangelist".
Both should be Bible teachers.
* The Bible teacher teaches the Bible to nurture spiritual life.
* The evangelist teaches the Bible to bring people to spiritual
  rebirth.
Where evangelists do not see themselves as Bible teachers
their evangelism is often shallow and unbiblical.

> **The Bible teaching in the programme is not like a pill
> which you are serving with jam. Imagine it more like this:**
> You are planning a new section of your garden.
>   You have always wanted to grow a small but beautiful
> tree – an Acer Brilliantissum.
>   You start to design that section of the garden to show
> off your lovely tree to its advantage.
>   You want to make sure that everyone who looks at
> the garden will immediately be drawn to the tree.
>   You want everything else in the garden to comp-
> lement it in colour and in shape.
>   So round the tree you leave some space. You know
> that the pale pink/green leaves will be enhanced by the
> brown soil.
>   Then you choose the other plants which will grow
> there – they will also need to be the right colour and
> shape so that attention is not deflected from the tree.
>   The whole of the new section of garden will be beauti-
> ful but in the middle, with pride of place, will stand
> the tree.

That is how it is with our Bible teaching. The other material in the programme is not there to make our teaching more palatable or to give the children something interesting after our boring spiel so that, against all the odds, they come back the next day. Not at all. Everything in the programme is there to enhance the centre-piece – the truth of the gospel. Around that we will provide space, other helpful and fun activities, but everything will be turning the attention of the children and the adults to that central beautiful focus point.

That is why we have said that the teaching programme will need careful planning from the beginning. Decisions will need to be made about what the teaching for the week should cover – remembering that children need to hear the whole truth and not a pulped version of it. Many of those children will not be from Christian homes nor from homes where the Bible is a familiar book. It is important that the teaching reflects this.

It is no longer a "jam and pill" situation. If we have our theology right we are thinking in terms of proclaiming the gospel, and living out the gospel of God. So we need to make sure the gospel is clear whether we are talking about it, or talking about kites; whether we are singing songs about God or one which makes everyone tie themselves up in knots; whether we are sharing a funny joke with them or explaining how we know that God keeps his promises.

Evangelism with children
is to live and talk the Christian life in such a way that the children know what the Bible says, understand what God is like and realise that the way to come to him and to live a full, satisfying life is to come to God through Jesus.

It is re-telling Bible events accurately and with a view to provoking and answering questions.

That's not "jam and pill" but rather "jam and nourishing wholemeal bread".

The programme we plan must reflect this attitude. It will have a specific point about what the Bible says about God which will be the focus of all the activities in the programme. It will clearly show in appropriate, memorable ways what the Bible says which God wants children to know. It will emphasize the fact that everything we say and are is because of who God is and what he says.

7.5 How do we use story-telling?

Story-telling is one of the most important skills to acquire – and it is never completely perfected. The Bible is not simply a book of stories but teaching it well depends on that skill.

The skill of story-telling is basic to communicating well to a group. The lack of that skill makes the task of the teacher doubly difficult. It is worth working hard to improve this skill.

Watch . . .
professional people who use story-telling on the television. Look at the expressions on their faces, the movements of their hands, the way they lean towards and away from their audience to create different moods and the way they use pictures.

Listen to . . .
the tone and pitch of their voice. Find out how they use their voice to indicate a change of scene, an increase in excitement, amazement or fear.

Copy . . .
as many of these skills of story-telling as possible. Read stories out loud from books and tell them from memory.

Experiment . . .
with real children as often as possible. Skills go stale and techniques are forgotten very easily. By experimenting and using the gifts you have regularly, the skill will grow.

Keeping the attention of the group through the gift of

story-telling is not enough in itself. Their aim needs to be very clear. Story-tellers are in the role of a teacher and there is a specific point they want to teach. The whole text of the talk should reach that one aim. The individual words need to be thought about and practised. They need to be memorised. Lie in the bath and talk to the taps. Go through the talk several times. Pick out the parts where you are floundering for the right words and think them through. Try them out loud until you find the right way to explain what you want to say. Then say it out loud several times so that it comes easily to mind.

Remind yourself all the way through your preparation time that this story really happened to real people. It fitted into its place in history and it stayed in the minds of the people who witnessed it to such an extent that they bothered to write it in a book. That means it really impressed them. Pray that the Holy Spirit will make the event more and more real to you as you study it. He was there at the time. Pray that by the time you have completed your preparation it will feel as though you had been there too and are drawing on your own memory of it as you tell it.

The same rules apply to talking to children as talking to any other group of people:
- Start by telling them what you are going to say.
- Then say it.
- Then tell them what you have said.

You will need to introduce the story in such a way that the main point is recognized when they hear it later; then tell the story accurately and with imaginative use of language and other story-telling skills. Then point out what the story is teaching. If you have introduced this at the beginning, and told the story accurately, the point will be obvious anyway – you are after all teaching what the Bible is teaching.

7.6 How do we use creative expression?

The God whose Gospel we will be explaining in our Bible teaching is a Creator God. He made people in his own image – that is why we are all creative people. The use of workshops in the programme not only offers the ideal way for children to enjoy showing how creative they are but also has all sorts of other benefits.

Choose the workshops to:
• reflect the interests of the children.
• use the gifts of the leaders.
• fit in with the theme of the event.

You could choose from:
art/craft, music, table games, energetic games, kite-making, parachute games, banner-making, puppets, drama, cooking, dried flowers, clay/dough modelling, dance, junk modelling, electronics, carpentry, video-making, computers, masks, video-watching.

There is no end to the list of possibilities.

Because God has made us creative people like him, the place of creative fun in the Bible-teaching programme is very important. Workshops offer opportunity for personal contact in a way few other activities do. The programme may allow the children to choose which workshops to go to at a certain time. Or the workshop may be an activity related to the theme which everyone does.

Either way the workshops offer:
• the opportunity for every leader to have a friendly, personal conversation with a child – to hear questions and suggest answers.
• the opportunity to pick up any way in which the event is worrying or difficult for the child to handle.

> - the opportunity for leaders to meet parents when they bring or fetch their child.
> - the chance for children to work side by side as they react to what they have heard and experienced.
> - the chance for leaders to observe children working creatively.

7.7 How do we make sure that our programme is balanced?
If you asked the under-tens in my church which parts of the video of our Easter Event they would like to see again, they would choose from "When Sheila got soaked in the rocket", "When the seagull splodged Geoff in the eye with shaving cream" or "When we had the baby fox and the chicks to visit us".

Should we feel disappointed about that? Perhaps we would prefer them to want to see the band play the theme songs or Wendy "doing the Psalm" or even one of the talks. I don't feel disappointed, because we do not see the programme as being divided into "jam and pill", unlike evangelism in a previous generation, which was seen as doing the serious stuff after the fun had stopped.

> It was generally accepted in education circles that "If you want to learn anything you have to be serious."
> **That was, in fact, never true**.
> We learn most from someone teaching us:
> - when what we are hearing makes us ask questions.
> - when what we are hearing is answering questions which we have already been asking.
> - when we are relaxed.

When we look at the endless possibilities for an interesting event for under-tens, the difficulty is to create a balance in the programme. The danger is that as we work on the programme it will be the parts which involve the most people, or which will be the trickiest to organize, which become the focus of our minds.

In that case we will find that we are adapting other items to fit in with them. They will become, by dint of quite wrong premises, the pivot on which everything turns.

It is important that the main aim of the whole event and of that particular day's programme is in front of you while you balance the programme. Otherwise, the teaching point for the day will be lost amongst a welter of lesser things.

Within a mission where the team visits schools during the day and then runs a club each afternoon, the club programme for under-tens might look like this:

3.35 **Show the Video**	made by those enjoying the club the day before.
3.43 **Band:**	Come and Jump Aboard. Jump on board. It's a new day – with sea video
Start	
Band:	It's a new day – learn and sing
3.45 **Welcome:**	Ann mention schools: St Stephen's Infants, Taverill Road Juniors, Cherry Lane Primary
3.48 **Drama Team:**	Misbehaviour by First Mate and Jasper with drums; take off by Captain Crucial.
Band:	Come and Jump Aboard. Jump on Board.
3.55 **Game:**	Pauline/Pete
4.05 **Band:**	Come on and let's praise. We are the children of the king. I will click.
4.10 **Dance:**	Introduced by David
4.15 **Psalm:**	Ann/Tim
4.20 **Treasure Hunt:**	Captain Crucial

4.25 **Drama/talk/**   team/Sally/Pam
song/prayer/booklet:
4.40 **Band:**   We are the children of the king.
4.45–5.30 **Workshops**

All this will be part of our evangelism programme because all of it is aimed at bringing every child another step along the pathway of their relationship with their Almighty God. Some of the items will need a lot of practical preparation and hilarious trial-runs. Others will involve hours spent studying the Bible and talking it through with other members of the team. All of it will need a lot of prayer and all of it will be under spiritual attack because all of it is proclaiming the Gospel of God.

With such a variety of programme, everything must be prepared beforehand. It is true that in some teaching situations you can plan to get equipment ready while your group of children is busy producing work related to what you have covered so far, but as you come down the age-levels this becomes less and less possible. One of the first shocks a student has in primary education is that "the children need you all the time".

Having a good, balanced programme is no good if we limp our way through it while we are trying to prepare equipment. The good programme is also wasted if we are not ready for a response from the children. Everything must be ready and tried out beforehand; everyone involved must know exactly what they are doing, who they are to take over from, what their cue will be and what their first sentence will be. If this level of preparation does not take place, discipline not evangelism becomes the leader's main concern.

7.8. What response will children make when the Bible is taught properly?

Whenever people are challenged about spiritual matters they need time to think and time to react. Few things are more frustrating and infuriating than to be deeply challenged about the personal implications of something in the Bible, and then to be asked to sing a "closing hymn" before being sent home.

Our traditional services have Bible teaching after some singing, prayer and reflection but allow no time for any of this
afterwards. I always feel I need as much time to respond
after the teaching as I need time to prepare for it beforehand.

Children need time to respond. This may be given in the
form of music to listen to, or a short time of silence with
some indication of the way they might pray. Those leading
may pray out loud to help the children put form to their
thoughts. In each case they need to explain that each child
will have a personal and unique reaction. The speaker is not
speaking to God on behalf of the whole group but only of
certain individuals who choose to be included. They need to
make it clear to the whole group that their prayer is appropriate for only some of the children – and that is all right. They
must help children who don't know whether to respond or
whether they have already done so.

Never put children in the frustrating situation of hearing
God speak and experiencing the challenge of his Holy Spirit,
yet not knowing what to do about it. That is not fair. It
leaves them with feelings of guilt and dejection without the
knowledge of forgiveness. That is not the place where God
wants any one of us.

Children need to have some sort of indication of what we
would welcome as an appropriate response *towards us*.

For example, there might be a booklet which has been
devised for the occasion.

In that case make sure they know:
• how to ask for the booklet,
• who to ask,
• when to ask.

There might be the opportunity to have a one-to-one
conversation with someone who will listen to their
questions.

In that case make sure they know:
• when that will be,
• how to make use of the opportunity.

7.9 How does the publicity prepare for a response?

As we have already seen, a child's response to anything will be governed to a large extent, by the attitudes of parents. If we want the child to be free to respond to the Gospel and to have the necessary encouragement for spiritual progress, we must bear the parents in mind continually. From the very beginning of our event we need to make sure that the parents know what we want to do – we want to tell their children about their Creator God; we went to tell their children what their Creator God says in his Word; we want to show their children the difference it makes when people listen to and obey what God has said in his Word.

If our feeling is that the parents will not send their children when we make our aims this clear, then we should not want their children to come. We must not operate as though we know better than the parents and can overrule their decisions – the children are the responsibility of the parents as far as God is concerned. Apart from anything else, if we operate any other way we place the children in a dilemma. So the publicity must make the situation clear.

The publicity must give the following information clearly:
> date, place, time (of start and finish), frequency if part of a series, contact phone number, age-group, activities planned, church connection.

Be encouraged to do this for the sake of the children, but it may benefit the parents too. When one mother used the phone number after a children's event in my church she was in some distress. She was not a church-goer and her son had come to the event with a friend from school. He had come home from the club one day to find chaos at home. His mother had suddenly lost a five-month pregnancy and was waiting for her sister to come to take her to hospital while her mother was waiting to give the children tea. Not understanding what was happening the little boy went up to his mum and put his arms round her. "Mum, it's all right – God does impossible things magnificently."

The mother was understandably flabbergasted at this and rang the name on the publicity as soon as she returned from hospital. She had had a proper conversation with her son by this time and had heard the whole story of Nehemiah and his impossible job. She was overwhelmed by the faith of her small son who still hung on to the fact that God works powerfully today. Because my name was on the publicity I had the opportunity for half an hour of sharing my faith and my own experience of that faith within the context of a miscarriage. It is worthwhile making sure that the publicity prepares parents for such a response in a child.

The information you give may look something like this:

Come along to

Spring Up

at St Clements Church, Almond Street, Connely
for children aged 5-10 years old
to enjoy:

- games and fun
- Bible stories
- things to make
- music
- things to do

Every day 4 - 5.45pm
from April 11th to April 15th

Any questions? Phone Pam Collins on 655 5054

Copies of the main publicity should be properly printed and displayed in public places like the local library, supermarket and post office, not just in school. The publicity you use in school will announce your event to children and will also keep the school informed so that they can reassure parents who inquire about it there. The publicity in the public thoroughfare will assure parents that this is an official, accredited event. If you have a few posters properly printed you can then photocopy them in reduced size for handbills or on A4 for schools. Never deliver posters for schools which are larger than A4 – they may look brilliant to you but few schools will find the space for them to be displayed. As my own school used to say to promoters, "We can always promise to put up posters – we can't promise that nothing will be put on top of them."

7.10 What part does prayer play in evangelism?

Prayer needs to surround and support the whole situation from the very beginning. Think of the people who have promised to pray as part of your team. Refer to them in that context so that everyone else begins to have that attitude about prayer. Refuse to allow people to say, "I can only pray." If people do not pray we are in a vulnerable position. People have come out of prayer groups for our school assembly teams saying, "I never realised before that prayer is such hard work."

In order to pray, people need to have information. It is very difficult to be committed to praying regularly for people and evangelism if the one praying knows no details – nor the results of those prayers. As soon as people agree to pray they need to have as much information as possible and this needs to be updated regularly. If there are many different people involved in the evangelism, try pairing up the people who are praying with the people who have promised to pray so that there is personal contact and the sharing of experience.

Urge your church to pray. Even if you feel that the ones who are likely to pray have already contacted you, the rest of the church still needs to be informed. They may not take up their responsibility to pray but they need to be informed and reminded that the responsibility is theirs. Giving information and asking for prayer are all part of the preparation to be done before the first steps are taken in evangelism.

7.11 Will I need painkillers?

Some of the issues for prayer will be personal ones. This is because as soon as we start to teach the Bible to bring children to new life in Jesus, there will be opposition to us. This may be in a direct form from parents, for example. It is more likely to come in subtle ways which we do not immediately identify as attack. We may find that our family life develops a new hassle factor overnight or in other subtle and personal ways life becomes hard grind. It is important that we do not immediately see everything as attack from Satan – some of it may be a result of ordinary life or our own stupidity. But it is certainly true that there will be attack.

The most important factor in this situation is our own walk and life with God. We may react to the difficulties by becoming bad-tempered or down-hearted. We may start to argue that we must be doing the wrong things and working in the wrong area because otherwise why is all this happening? The only sensible reaction is to turn to God and lean on him, spending more time with his Word and in prayer, talking and listening to him.

7.12 What do we learn from the Bible to help us with this?

When I remember my parents working in that tough village situation or people I know who are battling away in inner-city areas, I often find the story of the Sower helpful.

> "The farmer went out to sow his seed. As he was scattering the seed, some fell along the path; it was trampled on, and the birds of the air ate it up. Some fell on rock, and when it came up the plants withered because they had no moisture. Other seed fell among thorns, which grew up with it and choked the plants. Still other seed fell on good soil. It came up and yielded a crop, a hundred times more than was sown." (Luke 8:5–8)

If I'd been that farmer I would not have wasted my good seed on infertile land when I had other good land to sow it in. If I'd been God I would not have sent my dad to a village situation where his deep knowledge of God's Word and his undoubted gifts for teaching reached only a dozen people on Sunday evening for over ten years. But God is the Sower and he sows his good seed everywhere. Peter reminds us in 2 Peter 3.9 that God is wanting everyone to come to repentance. He does not want one of his loved creation to be out of relationship with him. So he will sow the seed throughout the world.

Mark follows the story of the Sower in chapter 4 with another which reminds us how little we ever know about spiritual harvest:

"This is what the kingdom of God is like. A man scatters seed on the ground. Night and day, whether he sleeps or gets up, the seed sprouts and grows, though he does not know how. All by itself the soil produces corn – first the stalk, then the ear, then the full grain in the ear. As soon as the grain is ripe, he puts the sickle to it, because the harvest has come." (Mark 4:26–29)

Sometimes in evangelism we become dispirited because we feel that we are sowing good seed under slabs of concrete. Our minds are saying, "What's the point?" as we look at children who are poor, dirty and unmotivated to learn anything; children who are frustrating every attempt to turn them into peace-loving citizens and who live in areas of our country which are bleak, grey and cheerless.

We have never been promised that our evangelism will be successful, although a child's obvious step of faith will be a tremendous encouragement. We have never been promised that it will be fun, although I can say that I have always found it totally addictive. We have never been told that we will be sent to proclaim the gospel only to those who are

most suitably equipped to respond to new initiative – it was
to go to the poor, imprisoned and disabled.

That second passage from Mark reminds us that we are
quite unable to recognize what is good soil and what is poor.
If the growth of the Kingdom of God is as unseen as Jesus
says, then we shall be unable to measure it from the outside.
We can't evaluate it as we would if we were opening a new
shop or local amenity. For this reason we listen closely to
the Sower. We may be directed to an area which is tough,
like my parents' village – and we may be asked to work
faithfully in those fields without ever seeing the harvest.

7.13 Is evangelism always worthwhile?
One inner-city church in Birmingham decided to run a Holiday Bible Club for the children aged seven to ten who lived
in the area. It was advertised in the high rise flats and local
schools and shops. The home team was expanded by friends
invited from other churches and the club ran for three after-
noons.

The area around the church is not thriving or colourful. It
is a part of the inner city of Birmingham which has been
forgotten by each succeeding set of city council officers. The
fifty children who came each day had a very short concentration span. The programme had to change every ten
minutes, and by the end of the week the leaders were exhausted. On the last night, the children were invited to come back
and to bring other members of their family for refreshments,
songs and chat. Many came – in fact the hall was full. Many
of the adults looked cynical and wary.

From that club, some of the children started to come to
church. They found out that the people there welcomed
them. The children sit in the service and when people pray
out loud, *they* pray out loud. They have learnt that that is
what people do in their church. When the small church
community walked around the streets of the area praying for
it, the children walked around the streets praying and singing too – they had learnt that that was what happened in
their church.

We can look at this handful of children and say that the

Holiday Bible Club was worthwhile but we still see only a part of what God is doing. In every child and in every leader there was the work of his Holy Spirit. God was working in all our lives before the Holiday Bible Club started and he still continues – he is the Sower and he sows good seed. It felt like sowing good seed under concrete to the team on that mission, but it will be great fun to meet up with some of those children in heaven – especially if their concentration span has increased.

◊ **Looking back**

Have a look at the area where you are living:

- What makes children's evangelism tough for you?
- Why are you concerned about doing it at all?
- How do the children in your area respond to stories from the Bible?
- How do they respond to dance, drama and music?

◊ **Looking forward**

In the next chapter we look into the most vital part of any sort of evangelism – the way in which the church cares for the person who has taken a new step of faith. The new step may be the first one in their faith in Jesus Christ. The new step may the next one in several which they have taken recently. It may even be the step back into the pathway of God which they had wandered away from. Whatever the step is, they need the church to encourage and care for them. Read all about it.

8

Providing Suitable Follow-Up

8.1 Why follow-up?

I swallowed hard to settle my churning stomach, gave a last look round the sunny dormitory, frantically prayed that when I found this woman she would be on her own and fled out of the door before I could change my mind. I had decided that I must tell someone that I had "become a Christian".

I gasped with amazement, because there she was, going across the landing just ahead of me. I called out her name in a squeaky shout and she turned to look at me, but still headed for the stairs. I leant over the bannisters as she ran down the stairs looking up at me. "You know what you said last night?" I shouted, "Well, I'm a Christian now." She reached the bottom of the stairs and looked delighted as she headed for the leaders' room door. "Wonderful," she called out and disappeared inside. Unfortunately, she never spoke to me about it again and neither did any other leader on that camp. What had happened in me needed to be followed up with a conversation with someone so that I really understood what had happened. That is always true.

Look at Jesus. When he hears of the traumatic events following his healing of the man who was born blind, Jesus goes to follow him up. We read in **John 9:35–41**:
"Jesus heard that they had thrown him out, and when he found him, he said, 'Do you believe in the Son of Man?'
'Who is he, sir?' the man asked, 'Tell me so that I may believe in him.'

Jesus said, 'You have now seen him; in fact, he is the one speaking with you.'
Then the man said, 'Lord, I believe,' and he worshipped him.''
Look at the apostle Paul. He was in no doubt of the need for careful and appropriate follow-up. He wrote at least thirteen detailed letters to do just that.

8.2 What is important?

I expect that because I came from a Christian family my camp leaders assumed that I would be taken care of. As a result, I struggled in my faith for years and frequently regretted the choice I had made. It was simply the appetite which the Holy Spirit had given me to read the Bible, and a deeply ingrained sense of duty, which led to any progress at all. Of course, if I had been from a totally unchurched family, I would have had quite different needs.

A mission will produce many different sorts of response:

- There will be children who as Christians need encouragement and want to confirm their walk with God.
- There will be children who have given Christianity no thought before and want to make an initial response to the love of Jesus.
- There will undoubtedly be children who have lots of questions and need to have a safe place to ask them and to hear the answers.

The follow-up for each of these categories needs to be different.

8.3 What are the aims?

To follow carefully behind each child as they take steps of spiritual growth requires imagination, sensitivity and clear spiritual aims. If any of these ingredients is missing, the follow-up will be inappropriate and therefore ineffective.

I was from a Christian home. What I needed on that camp was for someone to sit down and to explain to me what my relationship with God had been for the last thirteen years and how it had now changed. I needed to see that the difficulty I had with giving in to God's love resulted from my rebellion to my parents. Going God's way was like giving in to them and going their way too.

Our follow-up should bear in mind the huge gap between the churched and the unchurched in our modern world. Children from church know so much which we can take for granted when we are working with them all the time. Their knowledge of the Bible, the Trinity and the Church suddenly becomes vital breath when their lives are touched by the Holy Spirit. This reservoir is often empty when leading an unchurched child to faith. In follow-up, be aware from the beginning of the huge gap between unchurched and churched children – mind that gap.

Aims for follow-up will stem from your aims for evangelism and could be any or all of these:

1 To introduce all the children into existing groups in the church.
2 To link each child who asks for help to a leader for an afternoon.
3 To link each child who asks for help to a leader over an extended period of time – perhaps six months.
4 To include visits to the home of each child in the follow-up plans.
5 To keep contact with children over the period of a year by having "Event reunions" every three months – the final one promoting the following year's event.

. . . or others.

Remind yourself of the aims you made for the outreach:
– To help each child to understand something of the love of God.
– To provide individual spiritual care for each child.
– To open the church to the family of each child.

   – To open up a way for the whole family to come to church
   again later.

The aims you have will affect the plans you make, the
people you use and the way you work the plans through.
Everyone who is involved will need to know the aim otherwise you will be working in different directions. You will all
need to refer back to the aim during the time you are working
on follow-up, so that you keep a continual check that you
are not going off at a tangent onto activities which although
good, do not help achieve your aims. They will simply drain
your energy and time and may even confuse the children
you are nurturing.

So:
- Decide on your aims prayerfully.
- If you have more than one aim, put them in priority
  order.
- Make sure everyone who is involved is informed.
- Make sure that everyone involved agrees to work
  towards those aims.
- Check back to your aim continually while working
  through your plans.
- Praise God at the end as you realize that you have
  achieved your aims.

8.4 How much is practicable?

Our difficulty in following this growth in new Christians is
that there are so many different steps of faith. We simply
cannot presume that children will all be at the same stage at
the end of a mission, special event or holiday club. Each will
have started at a different stage varying from total lack of
spiritual awareness (or awareness of only its occult dimen-
sions) through to real Bible knowledge and a relationship
with God. At the end of the event all of the children and
leaders will have taken a step – perhaps several – of faith.
Some will have taken great long strides and run into the
Kingdom of God. Others will have tentatively put the next

foot forward. Each of them needs:
- to know what they have done,
- to be clear about where they are.
- to see an appropriate reaction in us.

So for those who have shown growth, we need to:
- *Show them that we do not know all the answers.* We must answer clearly questions which have a categorical biblical answer. We also need to make it clear when we are answering questions with our own opinions. The two kinds of answers are appropriate for different kinds of questions and we must be clear which kind of answer we are giving, otherwise children are not noticing the difference between us and God. This is not as unlikely as it sounds – many children put God/parents or God/teachers into the same category. Our answers must make the difference clear.
- *Show them the on-going questioning nature of our faith.* This is difficult but important. The Christian life is the tension between firmly held faith and awareness of ignorance. It is the tension between a deepening knowledge of what the gospel is and a heap of questions which grow in their complexity. Children need to know that we are in the same situation of tension as they are and that it is in fact a healthy situation of growth.

Where children have responded to a call to faith, we need to:
- *Give reassurance of God's full acceptance of them* just the way they are now. Some children present a sad picture of low self-image based on the opinion they hear expressed continually by parents, school staff and friends. Some overcome this opinion by presenting an over-confident image which makes it hard for them to admit to us that they are responding to God's

love. Every child needs to know that God accepts
them completely just the way they are now.

- *Show them what the Bible says about God's aims for them*.
  God is always drawing us into a closer relationship
  with himself. He is aiming towards the day when
  Jesus will present each of us faultless before him.
  This is reassuring for us – God is never going to give
  up on us. He has chosen us because of what he can
  do, not because of the promising material we are
  offering him.

- *Make sure they know the Holy Spirit has come to live in
  them*. God does not just go on forgiving them but
  comes to live his own life in them too. Our hope and
  assurance as Christians is the combination of these
  two facts.

**And for those who feel that they have tried it all before
and have failed we need to:**

- *Show them that God has planned to go on forgiving them*.
  He knew that they would fail. He never intended for
  them to be able to manage without his forgiveness
  or his Holy Spirit. God knows them and the world
  better than that.

- *Show them that they need to come again to God for his
  forgiveness and his Holy Spirit* – and they need to do it
  every day. It will never be any different.

8.5 What materials are available?

The materials which will be used for follow-up will need to
be planned, prepared and organized in the preparation time
for the evangelistic event. No leader will feel like tackling
preparation for follow-up groups, especially using new
material, just after finishing the main event. Nor will you
feel like dashing around leaders during the main event trying
to organize what is going to happen afterwards, when you

are all only just surviving the main event. Make the follow-up materials a main item on a planning meeting agenda early on in the general planning and delegate the overall responsibility for writing off for sample materials – or writing your own – so that everyone has time to look at it and to discuss it.

Look first of all at the material you use to teach the Bible to the groups of children already in your church. You may find that this is adaptable for children who are looking at the Bible for the first time. You will, of course, need to pick and choose the themes and passages which you would want a child with a new faith to delve into. There are advantages of using material in your special follow-up groups which the children are going to meet later when they come into the week-by-week life of your church. They will find the structure and approach familiar and this will be reassuring at a time when everything else could make them feel very much "the newcomers".

Decide first of all what main Bible teaching would be appropriate in these early weeks of faith and then look through your regular material to find anything which could be adapted. Next look at material which is produced especially with follow-up in mind.

Unfortunately there is a dearth of such materials for the age-group we are considering. The main organizations to write to for sample materials are:

Breakthrough Training Kit for leaders' training on follow-up: "Two Ways to Live", "Crossover", "On My Own Two Feet", from:

• CPAS,
     Athena Drive,
     Tachbrook Park,
     Warwick CV34 6NG

• Follow-up materials from:

- Follow-up materials from:
	Scripture Union, Missions Department,
	130 City Road,
	London EC1V 2NJ

- Ishmael, for "Father God I wonder":
	PO Box 198,
	Littlehampton,
	West Sussex BN17 6SP

8.6 How can we produce our own materials?

Look at the possibility of producing your own follow-up materials. The advantage of this is that at the end of the week, every child can go home with material which:

- reminds them of the Bible teaching they have received,
- gives another opportunity for the Holy Spirit to speak,
- gives them time to think quietly about what they have heard in the context of a large group,
- gives you the opportunity to tell parents what you want them to hear,
- gives parents the opportunity to come back to you by phone to discuss what their children have been talking about.

Here are some samples of the pages which could make up your booklet for the children to use after the main event. Remember when you plan it that this booklet can form the basis for the initial response a child makes during the event. For example, if you run a workshop where the children can ask questions, the booklet can be used to remind them of the material through the week and in this way provoke again the questions which have come into their minds. A sample page might look something like this:

PICTURE

God loved all the people in Nineveh.
Jonah thought God loved only special people.
God wants everyone to know that he loves them.
God loves you.
God wants you to know.

Have you told God that you know how much he loves
you?

yes/no

It might conclude with a prayer for children to use:

If you want to talk to God and you don't know what
to say, you could use these words:

Dear Father God,
  Thank you for making me.
  Please forgive me for doing things which make you
angry and sad.
  Thank you for sending Jesus so that you can forgive
me.
  Please send your Holy Spirit to live in my life all the
time.

Amen

The parents' letter might say something like this:

Note to parents:

This card has been given by Christian people from All
Saints Church, Flumton, to help your child understand
what God is like.

We want children and adults to know who Jesus is.
Please phone us if you have any questions – so that
you can help your child to understand.

contact: Sally Thompson 616 0361

8.7 How do I arrange for follow-up?
You need to gauge the arrangements already operating for
children in your church, in the light of the sort of evangelism
you are planning. Be honest with yourselves about the situation. To tell yourselves that your regular arrangements seem
successful simply because the groups are filled with churched
children whose parents insist they come week after week is
not being honest. You will then end up wondering how to
incorporate unchurched children into them after an exciting
Holiday Bible Club.

Decide what facilities you have for the sort of follow-up
you might need to run. Obviously, if you have only a
huge hall, with peeling paint, available one evening a
fortnight, this will influence the decision you make about
following up the spiritual growth of a group of six eight-
year-olds.

Here are three suggestions:
- The groups which form part of your weekly regular
  programme.
- Home groups which have been set up to operate
  long-term.
- A reunion for all the children who came to the main
  event.

8.8 How can we use our regular groups?
If evangelism is the normal life of any church, it seems
reasonable to expect the follow-up to fall naturally into the
pattern of nurture for children in the church. This can be

done but it certainly does not happen successfully without a decision being made about it. The regular group needs to acknowledge that children are joining it who are new in their faith, newcomers to the Bible, or even just beginning to think about spiritual things at all.

Come to

Explorer

every Sunday
10.30 - 11.30 am

at All Saints, Flumton,

to enjoy games,
friends and the Bible.

A check list is often a helpful thing especially if it is seen as a guideline rather than hard and fast rule. None of us lives in an ideal world under perfect conditions. The important thing is to assess the situation realistically. If the best follow-up is offered in our regular groups, decide to use them for that purpose.

This list gives the ideal conditions:
- If your regular groups are small.
- If your regular groups are not filled with children who know all the answers.
- If the groups have leaders who are committed to being in the group every time it meets.
- If the ratio of leaders to children means that you can realistically expect leaders to nurture a child who is new to faith.

> • If the groups are led by people who are clear about their faith and able to put faith into clear language.
>
> Of course, these are the ideal conditions for your regular groups anyway.

When your follow-up is to take place in the on-going work of your weekly groups, certain issues need to be clear. Leaders must know which child they are responsible for among those who have recently taken a new step of faith. They must be able to spend time talking to that child and be committed to praying for the child. They need to visit the child's home and get to know other members of the family in order sensitively to become the link between the life of the child at home and the life of the child at church. This is as vital for a child from a Christian home as for any other. It was this link which was missing at camp when I took that step of faith in my relationship with God.

They will also need help to plan their regular teaching programme with these new Christians in mind. It is hard to teach even a simple mathematical procedure to a group of people with a wide variety of experience, knowledge and understanding – let alone the Bible. It will be helpful if those who are taking this responsibility meet together to plan and pray. This is vital as children go through ups and downs of faith; no leader should be left feeling a sense of failure because a child has lost interest in coming to the group. Each of us has to take responsibility for our faith before God – it is actually unhelpful for the child to feel that leaders are avidly taking the child's spiritual temperature as a gauge of their own success.

It's easy to forget that this is still follow-up six months later. Leaders need to check progress with each other and also report back to the person who delegated the follow-up work to them, – the minister or vicar of their church, or perhaps the person who led the outreach event. If this was someone from outside, that person can be invited back to discuss the progress of individual children who came to faith through the event.

It is also important that the individual children know that you have remembered their situation. During your normal time with them, point out that it is six months since they joined the group. Listen to how they think that time has gone. Ask what they feel they are struggling with and what they are enjoying.

These points may well come up in conversation with some children regularly, yet it is good to show them how we take stock of our progress in our own Christian lives. This is good for the leaders too – it is quite hard to ask children about their progress in the last six months unless you have spent time assessing your own. The end product of this discussion should be assurance. The children need assurance that God has worked in their lives and is continuing to do so. Leaders need assurance that God has used them and will continue to work in their lives too.

8.9 How can we set up special home groups?
If your regular arrangements in the church cater for large numbers of knowledgeable children, it is better to plan follow-up separately. Recently, more people have been giving thought to the use of the home group system for children. If homes of members of your congregation are available near schools, this can be a vital and sensitive way to help those children who are either new to the faith or have a lot of questions about it.

These could operate on a weekly basis, but there is then the danger that they are seen as an alternative to the church groups and a bridge will never grow between the two. For this reason, it may be better to run the home groups regularly but infrequently – say once in each half term. Introduce the idea of these groups at the end of the main event and tell the children that they will be invited.

Nearer the time, give the children invitations, and also send a note to parents, explaining what will happen and saying the children will be picked up from the school gates.

Give them time to think about the idea and then on another

Come to

PRIVATE INVESTIGATORS

on Wednesday 30th June

at the home of
Tim and Lisa Holdard
20, Golders Road

phone 37 444

4 - 5pm

Tim and Liz are members of All Saints Church,
Flumpton

day, remind them of the arrangements to collect their
children from school. Be clear about what time you would
like them to be collected from your home and make sure that
the invitation has your name, address and phone number
clearly included on it. Find out what your own church leadership would like to have printed on the invitation which
would link this event firmly with your church.

The big advantage of this system of follow-up is that a
number of groups can cater for a wide variety of children
and, if they are kept to the ratio of ten children to every two
leaders, provide the ideal set-up for good conversation and
encouragement. As they can meet at any time during the
school term, there is no limit to the number of groups –
this is dictated by the number of pairs of leaders and their
homes.

The programme can follow the one suggested for home
groups (5.8). It could use other special follow-up material.
The same rules apply as before – that the parents of the
children need to know what you are planning to do and
what is involved in the invitation to the Home Group. You
may, of course, find the child removed from the group
because you have been open with the parents. That is their

prerogative. You may have an ideal opportunity to explain the Gospel in answer to the parent's questions.

In that case the spiritual life of the child will have a far bigger opportunity to grow and thrive.

8.10 How can we use a reunion?
The third type of event which can be used for follow-up is the big event. It may be more evocative of the original main event and because it is usually a one-off, it is easy to invite back any outside help you used then. It can be held in the same venue as before and can often be used not only to bring back the atmosphere and finishing point of the main event, but to start the publicity for the next one.

A big event is easier to resource with leaders because many of them will simply need to "turn up" and it is easy to make a venue attractive and decorative for one afternoon event. Having said that, it is limited in the spiritual aims which can be achieved. Admittedly, many children will be attracted to come but in terms of individual follow-up it will offer few opportunities.

Remember 'CrackPots'?

Come to a

CrackPot Reunion

on Saturday 31st May
at All Saints Church, Flumpton
from 2.30 to 5 pm

It will therefore be important, if you decide on a reunion, to make sure that individual follow-up and teaching are done at other times. Naturally, the possibilities for following up an event do not need to be limited to one type. Any mixture of these types can be used.

The big reunion will achieve different aims from the regular groups or the home groups.

- It gives a focus to all the groups in the church which cater for children. If you have groups which cater for new Christians, churched children, fringe members, this reunion brings them all together. This may well help you build the bridge you need between, for example, the home groups and the regular groups in the church.

- It provides motivation for your regular leaders and involves others who may gain their first taste of children's evangelism. These people will then be a source of new leaders for your next main event.

- It reminds the rest of the church about the work which is being done on their behalf for the children in their parish. This is often forgotten by the rest of the congregation. A big event demands some attention – and money – from those who are not involved.

- It gives the opportunity for children who are new Christians to invite their friends to hear the gospel. Many children have a hard time in primary schools as they try to use a new vocabulary to explain their new faith. This is a chance for them to invite their friends to meet the people and hear the teaching which have caused such a change in their lives.

The reunion needs to have a sharply focused aim otherwise it quickly deteriorates into "Let's remember CrackPots". It needs plenty of fun and colour – that's what the children will expect. However, there needs to be:

- *The opportunity for worship* – not just the singing of songs. Many of the children will be growing in their understanding of worship. This event needs to furnish them with songs/dance/scripture which they can use in their worship on their own at home.

- *The opportunity to chat*. At some time in the programme there will need to be an activity which requires small groups. Here children can express some of the joys and difficulties which their growth of faith has brought. The reunion should not be such a celebration that their stories of difficulties feel out of place. Your aim for their faith is a path of steady progress and growth. If you ignore their real situation in the reunion, they will start to live a pattern of struggle interspersed with spurious celebration.

- *The opportunity to renew relationships* with adults which started during the main event. They may have been disappointed by the particular adults who are leading their home groups. Perhaps during the event they were friends with quite different adults. Allow time for them to enjoy the adult Christians whose company they would really choose.

- *The chance to think again.* Some of them will look back on the event as the time when they understood the gospel but decided they were not ready for the sort of demands God was making. This is the opportunity to remind them of what God says – to give them time and space to think again.

8.11 How can we choose and prepare leaders to do follow-up?

The leaders you choose for follow-up will need careful preparation because they are less likely to feel they are members of a team. Care is needed when leaders are to work together in pairs – children will quickly pick up when there is friction or unease between them. If you are using male and female leaders, special care needs to be taken not only to partner people but to pastor them in their work and to make arrangements right from the beginning of the procedure to use in case of difficulties.

Look at the leaders you have regularly available. There may be people in your congregation who are free for one week a year by making special arrangements but who, for family or work reasons, could not be available on a weekly basis. It is worth making a simple survey of the availability of people in the church who would be good value in the follow-up.

You may find that there are three groups of people:

- those who are available on a weekly basis.
- others who could be available for a special event three times a year
- another group who could run a follow-up group twice a term after school.

The pattern of leaders' availability will be different in each area – but you need to know that pattern before you start any evangelistic effort. It will affect the follow-up plan.

Guidelines for follow-up using home groups with trained leaders:

- Provide the material centrally. Work out a programme which will be suitable for the time allowed. One hour is probably about right but ask the parents to come after another quarter of an hour to allow children time to chat, finish off craft and so on.
- Pair leaders comfortably together – they will need to be mutually supportive, approach children in a similar way and not be the sort who irritate each other on sight.
- Within each home group programme, plan a variety of activity so that there is time for them to learn and time for them to talk.
- Collect all the leaders together for an hour with a cup of coffee at the beginning of the school term. Go through all the material with them. Explain the Bible teaching, words and terminology you would use, play the game and show them how to make the craft. Leave time in this session:
  - for you to affirm and encourage them in what they are doing,
  - for them to pray together in pairs about the groups.
- Ask them to inform you as soon as possible when their groups will be held. Make sure they know how to collect their invitations from you. Make sure they know when you will deliver their materials. They

will need them about two days before the group
meets so that they have time to feel confident with
the programme.

- Arrange to collect the materials from them after the
group has met and try to do this in an unhurried
way so that the leader has time to talk about the
group. Even though you may not know the individual children involved, the leader needs to talk
about them – there will be certain details which will
be very clear in their minds to pray about once they
have talked it out to someone else.

8.12 How do we follow up the leaders too?

It is vital to realize that the children are not the only ones
who will react and respond to your main event. When God
works he does not follow an agenda which we have set
for him. Many leaders find themselves confronted by an
awesome, holy and loving God as they present him truthfully
to children or as they hear another leader doing so. It is
important that this confrontation and response are not shelved as being inappropriate simply because the event has
been billed for children. God is there and he does not work
in the neat compartments we would prefer.

Ideally there needs to be someone whose job is to
pastor the team
throughout the evangelism. If this relationship is good
and wide open then leaders will have someone who
will be involved in the follow-up they need. If God
speaks to us and we do not listen or we shelve the
matter continually until another time, then we become
spiritually deaf and immune to the presence of God.
This is a spiritually disastrous situation and certainly
does not promise well for the next main event.

You may find that a leader will initiate a conversation with you on a particular subject: "I've never thought about the cross like that before." Resist the temptation to answer, "Well, how on earth *have* you thought of the cross then?" Try to be open, not shocked, if a simple conversation like this reveals a lamentable lack of Bible knowledge. We have already said that people offer to help with children's work for a wide variety of reasons. If through this event they reach out for growth themselves, encourage them.

Talk with them briefly as well as you can in a situation where there may be a crowd of children. Certainly make the opportunity for a proper conversation as soon as possible – not weeks later when the whole matter may well have been shelved. Think in your own preparation and planning of books which deal with different issues likely to be raised in leaders' minds by the teaching you are giving the children. Have some spare copies ready to lend to leaders who respond in this way.

8.13 What about me?

The other leaders are not the only ones who will hear God's Word. You will too. Even though you may be fitting in two nervous breakdowns a day during the main event, God's Word will be heard and you will respond. Be ready for that and welcome it. But be warned that you need following-up too. Before the main event ever happens, ask someone who will be praying for you to act as your sounding board during the event so that you can speak out and hear how you are reacting. Then arrange to use that person afterwards to follow you up.

Your praying friend ought to want to know:
What have you learnt about God, Father, Son and Holy Spirit, which you have never known or temporarily forgotten?
How have you responded to that?

What has encouraged you most in your dealings with leaders?

What has encouraged you most in your dealings with children?

Has anything changed because of this?

How has your relationship with God been changed by this event?

How can I pray for you now that the event is over?

8.14 Communicate with everyone

It is important that everyone knows the arrangements for follow-up – who is involved, when it is taking place, what materials are being used. Ideally these arrangements should be in printed form so that a written invitation can be given to children who are interested. This is true even if the invitation is simply to the normal groups to which the church children already come.

The leaders should also know that you are expecting everyone to respond in some way to what has been going on – that it is entirely natural for a leader to respond to God in a children's event. That, in fact, you are expecting to do that yourself.

◊ **Don't wait**

Please don't wait for this all to happen before you reach out to the children in your area with evangelism. When you work or live with children you realize continually how brief childhood is. You may sit rocking your baby in the middle of the night feeling that this pattern of broken nights will go on forever – then suddenly find that you are needing to discuss secondary or further education – childhood has gone. I look at our church youth group and realize that I have cared for most of them either in church groups or as a teacher in a local school. Now suddenly they are young adults – childhood has gone.

One of my sons needed comfort when he was three because his daddy had gone away on business for three weeks. He asked me about how God would look after us and stop us feeling sad and lonely. I tried to explain – then before I knew it we were talking about personal faith in a way I would have sought to avoid with a three-year-old. He pressed me with further questions and I backed off, all the time thinking, "He's too young. How did I get myself into this mess? What can I say to get his mind off the subject?"

I must have indicated that this would be something he would want to think about when he was older. He looked at me for a moment with that disconcerting straight look which a three-year-old can give. Then he tucked his teddy-bear upside-down under his arm and said with great finality, "Well, I can't wait till then – I'll tell Jesus now." I was not allowed to leave the room until he had.

There are a lot of children out there in the real world. Many of them are struggling with problems of our society which would make us flounder. Most of them know no Christian person and have no contact with any church. Few of them have access to the fact that God loves them and longs for their company.

It's no good leaving the telling of the gospel until you feel you have that perfect team successfully trained with the right resources and skills. It's no good telling people who are children now, that in five years' time when you've finished the building project and paid for the new organ you'll come to them with the gospel. In the words of my son they would say, "Well, I can't wait till then."

9

Resources

- There are many sources of help and advice for those working with children in and out of the church. Names and addresses are included in this chapter as a checklist.
- This chapter also lists some of the books which have helped me along the way. Some teach about theology, some offer help with practical skills. Some are books which I've found stimulating on a quick read through, while others are those to which I turn regularly for encouragement and help.
- At the end of the chapter is an audit to use when assessing the situation in your area before you dive into a new initiative in evangelism.

Useful Addresses:–
1 CPAS, Athena Drive,
   Tachbrook Park,
   Warwick
   CV34 6NG

   Tel: 0926 334242

CPAS is an Anglican home missionary society committed to evangelism, training and the support of workers in the local church. A wide range of resources is available through their sales unit, many of which are in the recommended list. Many audio-visual resources can be hired. CPAS has a particular concern for children and young people. Ring for a catalogue or write for parish advice and consultation.

2 Scripture Union
 130 City Road
 London
 EC1V 2NJ

 Tel: 071 250 1966

Scripture Union is an international, interdenominational society. There are over 25 bookshops in Britain where all of the publications and audio-visual resources can be purchased. Many of the shops also offer a hiring facility. All items are available through mail order (enquiry number 0272 771131). The hiring of videos and soundstrips is from SU Hire Orders, 9–11 Clothier Road, Brislington, Bristol BS4 5RL

3 In Contact Ministries
 St Andrew's Road
 Plaistow
 London
 E13 8QD

In Contact Ministries specializes in work among the Asian and other ethnic communities in inner-city areas of Britain. It is concerned with evangelism and caring, and provides training for those working in these areas. Conferences and training courses are held at the St Andrew's Centre and in churches throughout the country. In Contact also have information about all other societies and churches working in Asian and other ethnic communities throughout Britain.

4 CLC Asian Literature Department
 51 The Dean
 Alresford
 Hampshire
 SO24 9BJ

A range of Christian literature, including tracts and gospels, is available in a number of Asian languages.

5 Christian Publicity Organization (CPO)
  Garcia Estate
  Canterbury Road
  Worthing
  West Sussex
  BD13 1BW

  Tel: 0903 64556

On request CPO will send a catalogue and samples of their materials. You can also be placed on their mailing list to receive samples of new materials and the annual catalogue.

6 Palm Trees Press
  Rattlesden
  Bury St Edmunds
  Suffolk
  IP30 052

The Instant Art series of books are ideal for assisting the production of DIY publicity, newsletters and magazines. These are available in most Christian bookshops.

Many local Christian bookshops are outlets for the sale of Christian videos. Some offer a hiring service. An increasing number of national organizations are making hiring facilities available through mail order. The procedure is simple and in most cases inexpensive, making videos more accessible to Christians engaged in evangelistic work. Here are three organizations which offer this hiring service:–

7 Gospel Vision
  143 Toller Lane
  Bradford
  West Yorkshire
  BD89 9HL

  Tel: 0274 54137

8 Christian World Centre
  Box 30
  123 Deansgate
  Manchester
  M60 3BX

  Tel: 061 834 6060

9 International Films
  235 Shaftesbury Avenue
  London

  Tel: 071 836 2255

Books

Real children:

Roger Owen, *Parents 5–11 Guide*, Kingsway Publications 1988

Jean Watson, *Happy Families*, Hodder and Stoughton 1983

Brenda Crowe, *Your child and you*, Unwin, London 1986

Pat Wynne-Jones, *Pictures on a Page*, Lion Publishing 1982

Zig Ziglar, *Raising Positive Kids*, Highland Books, 1986

James Dobson, *Hide or Seek*, Hodder 1982

Shirley Leslie, *Children Growing Up*, Scripture Union 1982

Susan, Macauley Schaffer, *For the Children's Sake*, Kingsway 1986

Jeremie Hughes, *Will my rabbit go to heaven?* Lion Publishing 1988

Phoebe Cranor, *Why did God let Grandpa die?* Bethany Fellowship, Minnesota 1976

E. M. Matterson, *Play with a Purpose for Under-Sevens*, Penguin 1975

John Bowlby, *Child Care and the Growth of Love*, Pelican 1965

D. W. Winnicott, *The Child, the Family and the Outside World*, Pelican 1964

Susanna Millar, *The Psychology of Play*, Pelican 1968

Real evangelism:

Michael Green, *Evangelism Now and Then*, Inter-Varsity Press

Michael Green, *Freed to Serve*, Hodder and Stoughton

Michael Green, *Evangelism through the local church*, Hodder and Stoughton 1990

Michael Green, *Baptism*, Hodder and Stoughton 1987

J. C. Aldrich, *Lifestyle Evangelism*, Multnomah Press

Board of Mission and Unity, *The Measure of Mission*, Church House Publishing

Board of Education, *Children in the way*, Church House Publishing

Board of Mission and Unity/Education, *All God's Children?*, Church House 1991

John Chapman, *Know and Tell the Gospel*, NavPress

Peter Cotterell, *Church Alive*, Inter-Varsity Press

Val Grieve, *Your Verdict*, Inter-Varsity Press

Paul Little, *How to give away your faith*, Inter-Varsity Press

Paul Little, *Know Why You Believe*, Scripture Union

Josh McDowell, *Evidence which demands a verdict* Campus Crusade

Rebecca Manley Pippert, *Out of the Saltshaker*, Inter-Varsity Press

David Watson, *I Believe in Evangelism*, Hodder and Stoughton

John White, *The Fight*, Inter-Varsity Press

Real world:

Neil Postman, *The Disappearance of Childhood*, W. H. Allen, London 1982

Maureen O'Connor, *How to help your child through school*, Harrap 1990

William Coleman, *What Children Need to Know*, Bethany House 1983

Pat Wynne-Jones, *Children, Death and Bereavement*, Scripture Union 1985

David Porter, *Children at Risk*, Kingsway 1986

David Porter, *Children at Play*, Kingsway

Robert Hemfelt and Paul Warren, *Kids who carry our pain*, Word Books 1991

Francis Bridger, *Children Finding Faith*, Scripture Union

Ron Buckland, *Children and God*, Scripture Union

Real God:

John White, *When the Spirit Comes in Power*, Hodder and Stoughton

John Stott, *Basic Christianity*, Inter-Varsity Press

J. I. Packer, *Knowing God*, Hodder and Stoughton

Colin Chapman, *The Case For Christianity*, Lion Publishing

Graeme Goldsworthy, *Gospel and Kingdom*, Paternoster Press 1981

Settings for evangelism:

John Hattan, *Family Evangelism*, Scripture Union

Peter Grayson, *Help, there's a child in my church*, Scripture Union

Choosing, training and leading the team:

TeamTalk, Available from CPAS

Gordon D. Fee, *1 and 2 Timothy, Titus*, New International Biblical Commentary

Doing evangelism:

Maggie Durran, *All Age Worship*, Angel Press

Elspeth Stevenson, *Tell it to Jesus*, Scripture Union

When you pray with 3–6s, National Christian Education Council

Michael Lush, *Know How – all-age activities for learning in worship*, Scripture Union

Howard Mellor, *Know How – to encourage family worship*, Scripture Union

Michael Botting, *For All The Family*, Kingsway

Steve Hutchinson, *Operation Barnabas*, Scripture Union

Steve Hutchinson, *Help! I want to tell kids about Jesus!*

Teaching materials:

trek – for ages 3s–6s, 7s–10s, available from CPAS

Learning Together – 5s–7s, 7s–10s, available from Scripture Union

Children/Young People and Evangelism Audit:
This audit is to help you think through the situation in your
church and your local area regarding children and young
people. Only then can you assess what evangelism is possible
and appropriate.

**Consider what information you have about children and
young people in your community:**
What ethnic and religious groups are represented?
Are there any schools or centres for the young with special
needs?
What are the local statistics regarding
– single parent families
– unemployment overall
– unemployment among young people

What is the way in which most parents use their free time?
What facilities are available for them?

What is the way in which under-10s use their free time?
What facilities are available for them?
How do the facilities change in the school holidays?

How do you suppose teenagers use their free time?
What facilities are available for them?
How do the facilities change in the school holidays?
What sort of schools are in the area?
What proportion of teenagers leave school at 16?
How many have to travel some distance to school/college or
work?

Look then at the Under-5s:

What is the present state of their activities in your church?
With regard to
• leaders:
  How many?
  Of what type?
  With what aims?
  With what attitude toward family evangelism?
• under 5s:

How many regular attenders?
Are they all from linked families?
- space/rooms available?
- family evangelism going on already?
- materials/resources?
- budget?

What is the present climate among your under-5s?
(You'll find this out by listening to them when they are on their way to their activities – do they go with pleasure and anticipation?)
Do they find church and Christianity:–
    boring / irrelevant / a time-filler / fun / vital and interesting?

Be honest!
- When under-5s come into your mind what is your first reaction?
- What is the attitude of your congregation towards under-5s?
- Would there need to be change in the existing arrangements for under–5s if many more arrived in the present groups as a result of family evangelism?
- What are other Christian groups doing for under–5s in the area?

Look then at the 5s–10s
What is the present state of their activities in your church with regard to
- leaders:
  How many?
  Of what type?
  With what aims?
  With what attitude to children's/family evangelism?
- 5s–10s:
  How many regular attenders?
  Are they all from linked families?
- space/rooms available?
- children/family evangelism going on already?
- materials/resources?
- budget?

What is the present climate among your 5s–10s?
(You'll find this out by listening to them when they are on their way to their activities – do they go with pleasure and anticipation?)
Do they find church and Christianity:
  boring / irrelevant / a time-filler / fun / vital and interesting?

Be honest!
- When 5s–10s come into your mind, what is your first reaction?
- What is the attitude of your congregation towards 5s–10s?
- Would there need to be change in the existing arrangements for 5s–10s if many more arrived in the present groups as a result of children/family evangelism?
- What are other Christian groups doing for 5s–10s in the area?

Look then at the 10s–18s
What is the present state of their activities in your church with regard to
- leaders:
  How many?
  Of what type?
  With what aims?
  With what attitude to evangelism?
- 10s–18s:
  How many regular attenders?
  Are they all from linked families?
- space/rooms available?
- evangelism going on already?
- materials/resources?
- budget?

What is the present climate among your 10s–18s?
(You'll find this out by listening to them when they are on their way to their activities – do they go with pleasure and anticipation?)
Do they find church and Christianity:
  boring / irrelevant / a time-filler / fun / vital and interesting?

Be honest!
- When 10s–18s come into your mind, what is your first reaction?
- What is the attitude of your congregation towards 10s–18s?
- Would there need to be change in the existing arrangements for 10s–18s if many more arrived in the present groups as a result of evangelism?
- What are other Christian groups doing for 10s–18s in the area?

And finally and realistically:
What would be readily available as extra resources for an evangelistic event for children and young people in terms of:
   money / expertise / facilities / resources / training?
What other expenditure could be cut to release more money for this?